BRAND MARKETING

Building Winning Brand Strategies That Deliver Value *and* Customer Satisfaction

William M. Weilbacher

NTC Business Books
a division of *NTC Publishing Group* • Lincolnwood, Illinois USA

Library of Congress Cataloging-in-Publication Data

Weilbacher, William M.
    Brand marketing /William M. Weilbacher.
        p.   cm.
    Includes index.
    ISBN 0-8442-3476-1
    1. Brand name products — Marketing.   2. Brand choice.   I. Title.
    HF5415.15.W425 1993
    658.8'27 — dc20   92-20338
                                                                                          CIP

Published by NTC Business Books, a division of NTC Publishing Group
4255 West Touhy Avenue
Lincolnwood (Chicago), Illinois 60646–1975, U.S.A.
© 1993 by William M. Weilbacher. All rights reserved.
No part of this book may be reproduced, stored in a retrieval system,
or transmitted in any form or by any means,
electronic, mechanical, photocopying, recording or otherwise,
without the prior permission of NTC Publishing Group.
Manufactured in the United States of America.

3 4 5 6 7 8 9 BC 9 8 7 6 5 4 3 2 1

For Sweets
(Not the trumpet player)

Foreword

by RANDALL ROTHENBERG

A half-century after the Existentialists informed us that life has no purpose and 30 years after a band of renegade theologians told us that God is dead, William Weilbacher has come along to retail perhaps the most alarming pronouncement yet on the American way of life: Marketing has no meaning.

Yes, I know what you're thinking. If marketing has no meaning, why did Sears *and* Nordstrom *and* Stern's pay who-knows-how-many-kazillions-of-dollars per square foot to anchor the new local shopping mall? If marketing has no meaning, why did American Express fire Ogilvy & Mather, hire Chiat/Day/Mojo, and then put pressure on Chiat/Day/Mojo by hiring Ogilvy & Mather to produce a new set of American Express Card commercials? If marketing has no meaning, why does shopping for an analgesic give me such a headache?

Which is exactly Bill Weilbacher's point.

Before I provide the customary explanation and praise that readers expect in such introductions, I feel it my duty to lay out the credentials that allow me to dispense this Talmudic commentary.

I have none.

Perhaps Mr. Weilbacher thought choosing an unscholarly non-professional was a clever way of circumventing scrutiny of his thesis, research, and analysis.

If so, he was wrong. For although I cannot boast the senior vice presidency of an advertising agency or a brand management position at Unilever on my resumé, I spent enough years in the presence of such greats and near-greats (in my capacity as advertising columnist and media reporter at *The New York Times*) to know that the chatty but orderly book you hold is a full-throttled assault on the conventional wisdom held dear in the hallowed precincts of marketingdom. And I also know that Mr. Weilbacher — the former director of research at Dancer-Fitzgerald-Sample, an advertising consultant whose clients have included Prudential, Burger King, and other giant corporations, and a man whose previous books include the definitive work on how to find an advertising agency — has enough credentials for the two of us. Or for the three of us, if I may be so bold as to include you, dear reader, in this discussion.

For it is *you* to whom this book is most specifically addressed. Chances are, you are a marketing manager or other senior corporate executive wondering why you're having such trouble maintaining Cheesy Lites's market share after its prominent launch two years ago. Or, you're a junior exec frothing at the mouth, just waiting for the chance to replace the geezer who blew the Cheesy Lites intro. Maybe you're an ad agency rain-maker looking for some clue about snatching the Cheesy Lites account from the creative boutique that has it now. or it might be that you're a first-year M.B.A. candidate hoping for help in landing a summer job in the Cheesy Corp.'s snack-foods division, your first-choice employer — Drexel Burnham Lambert providing more work for investigative reporters than rocket scientists these days.

If you belong to any of these groups (or if you're simply an average shopper, wondering why the semi-weekly trip to Grand Union increasingly seems like a plunge through the looking glass) you must read on. For in investigating what these days is routinely called "the marketing crisis," Mr. Weilbacher has interviewed and dismissed the usual subjects: self-indulgent advertising agencies, a bedraggled economy, bad television pro-gramming, a fragmented audience. Instead, he lays the blame squarely on the mahogany credenzas of the nation's C.E.O.s and their marketing directors. Because of laziness, short-term thinking, uninspired marketing re-search, and a penchant for financial manipulation instead of innovation, they and their corporations are flooding our stores and minds with meaningless brand extensions.

Mr. Weilbacher's message, in short, is direct and remorseless: Cheesy Lites probably should never have existed in the first place.

This is heresy, of course. It is commonplace to attribute the continued prosperity of Procter & Gamble (to pick on the biggest, meanest, and most boring of our packaged-goods manufacturers) to Tide, Liquid Tide, Tide Ultra, scentless Tide and the — oh, I don't know — 1.74 billion line extensions bearing the Tide name. After all (so goes the conventional wis-dom) these "flanker" products meet the desires of the millions of consumers for whom plain, powdered laundry detergent just won't do. These are the women and men — I'm sure we all know several dozen — who would un-doubtedly let their clothes stay dirty if they couldn't buy a super-powered liquid detergent that smells like some junior high school chemistry student's version of lemons.

And let us not forget (continues the conventional wisdom) that flankers protect valuable shelf space in the supermarket, keeping the Tide name front and center, lest Wisk or some other evil interloper steal the consumer's share of mind.

Hogwash, Mr. Weilbacher maintains. Consumers are far less stupid than brand managers. The proof? They couldn't care less about the products they're marketing. In fact, shopping (or "brand choice," as the eggheads call it) is so far below the interests of the vast majority of Americans that it's not even a rational process. Not that it's irrational, mind you. As Mr. Weilbacher tells it, shopping doesn't even dignify a trip into the subconscious. Take that, Ernest Dichter!

So most line extensions attract nobody, because their differences from other extensions of the brand (and from competitors in their category) are negligible to the point of insignificance. The support these extensions require drains the corporation's financial and creative resources, provides the retailer even more opportunity to demand slotting allowances and other trade promotions, and forces manufacturers into a spiral of price discounting that diminishes whatever power the brand's name once had. Faced with, at best, higher expenses in maintaining current market share or, at worst, share slippage, marketers make willy-nilly changes in their advertising strategy, or fire their advertising agencies (are you listening, Maxwell House?), further destroying a brand's identity.

It's a sordid tale, told by Mr. Weilbacher with elegance and economy — no mean feat in a field notable for its lengthy blather.

In making his case against the senseless padding of our grocers' shelves, the author takes on some of the hallowed icons, specific and general, of marketing lore. He dismantles the revered advertising campaigns for Alka-Seltzer by both Doyle Dane Bernbach and Wells, Rich, Greene. He dares to criticize aspects of John Smale's stewardship of Procter & Gamble. He takes on "Burke's Law" — recall testing and other bogus indicators of advertising effectiveness. He attacks his own area of specialization, terming marketing research a "collaborator in causing the business problems" of today. He calls most market segmentation research a futile, impractical exercise (and quotes the paleontologist Stephen Jay Gould in doing so, certainly a first!). And he blames clients for the failures of their ad agencies, attributing the "long-term decline in advertising creativity" to the "long-term decline in brand advertisability."

Finally, Mr. Weilbacher excoriates the ultimate villain in the melodramatic fall of the "marketing concept": the overarching desire for stability and predictability inside the corporation. Like the late economist Joseph Schumpeter, he maintains that innovation and success — both corporate and national — require a quest for disequilibrium, disharmony, and "creative destruction."

Bill Weilbacher's iconoclasm is unusual, but not singular. Like Leo Bogart, another respected marketing researcher and the longtime executive vice president of the Newspaper Advertising Bureau, Mr. Weilbacher is an unabashed believer in the power of creativity in advertising and marketing ... and an adherent to the view that creativity is messy, undefinable, ineluctable, and necessary for both product development and advertising execution. Like Jay Chiat, the head of an irreverent ad agency with which a man of Mr. Weilbacher's sobriety would not seem to be associated, he is a fan of account planning, the marketing research system imported from Britain which sets up researchers as the consumer's advocate in the advertising planning process. Mr. Weilbacher is also part of an influential clique that has assembled around the British statistician Andrew S.C. Ehrenberg (John Philip Jones of Syracuse University is another member), which holds that brand loyalty is a chimera; consumers, they say, do not blindly purchase the same brands over and over, but maintain a repertoire of acceptable brands in any category and move freely from one to another within their consideration set.

I raise these names not to impugn Bill Weilbacher's originality, but to show that his thinking—although not mainstream, in the boardroom-Harvard Club-Wharton School sense—is growing in acceptance, even as American marketing seems to be tumbling ever deeper into the Black Hole of Sameness.

Given this downward spiral, is innovation still possible? Mr. Weilbacher ends on a hopeful note. Unilever, he points out, finally managed to combine a deodorant soap and a moisturizing soap in one bar; just a few years after its launch, Lever 2000 is already cleaning up. (The pun wasn't intended, but now that I've recognized it, I think I'll keep it.) I know, I know... a hermaphroditic soap is not like sending a human being to Mars. But they said it couldn't be done; the task had eluded the greatest minds of soap-making for generations. Can true innovation in laundry detergent be far behind? In shampoo? In mayonnaise? Only time and tuna salad will tell.

So crack open that bag of Cheesy Lites and start learning. Better yet, why not go for the regular Cheesies? Sure, they're old fashioned. But they're better for you.

Randall Rothenberg is a fellow at the Freedom Forum Media Studies Center at Columbia University.

Contents

Introduction

This is a book about how brand marketing strategies go wrong and how to make them right.

The goal in marketing products or services is to create distinctive consumer satisfaction. Brand marketing strategy determines exactly what the corporation will *do* to create products or services that provide distinctive consumer satisfaction.

Contemporary marketing is plagued by its frequent failure to create brands that routinely provide distinctive consumer satisfaction. When a brand provides no more satisfaction to a consumer than does its competitors, it is a commodity. The destiny of commodities is not determined by marketing skill — it is determined by market price.

Many contemporary marketing practices contribute to distinctionless brands, and they will be discussed in the following pages. However, brand marketing's strategic failure is less a matter of individual marketing practices than a lack of fundamental understanding of what marketing must do to create satisfied customers.

Marketers generally do a good job of addressing the day-to-day problems of marketing: advertising, promotion, product development, trade relations, brand management, and the rest. But success in marketing does not come from the sum of superior performance with individual marketing activities. It comes from an *overall* vision of what the consumer wants or can be made to want from a product or service and how to deliver it. There is a lot more to this than simply running a consumer research project to find out what consumers are saying they want today and then doing what the research says to do.

A brand is a singular, global concept. It succeeds if consumers perceive it to be better than competitive brands. It fails if consumers do not so perceive it. As long as marketing is practiced as a collection of individual activities, each an end in itself, the development of singular, monolithic brands that satisfy lots of consumers most of the time will continue to be a daunting task for marketers.

I began thinking about this in earnest a couple of years ago while shopping in a nearby supermarket. I came upon a couple — well-dressed, alert-looking, possibly in their late forties. They appeared to me to be everything that a marketer could want in potential customers, and more.

This couple was doing their best to buy a bottle of Bayer aspirin. There was no doubt that their brand choice had long since been made; they were looking only at the array of Bayer brand variants. But they were clearly puzzled about which Bayer brand variant to buy. There were eight on the shelf, each with different modifying descriptors and each with apparently

different characteristics. One of the Bayer variants was offered by the retailer at a "special" price, yet it still was priced somewhat higher than the
other variants. In addition, five of the Bayer variants had a package flag
explaining that either the product or the package label itself was "new."

As I observed, the consumers examined each of the versions of Bayer
aspirin with considerable care, apparently unaware that the active ingredient
and thus the basic promise of therapeutic satisfaction was identical for each.
After two or three minutes they were clearly frustrated in their search. They
finally shrugged their shoulders at Bayer and moved to other brands in the
analgesic display. In the end, they purchased a bottle of regular Bufferin,
which apparently appeared less ambiguous and/or threatening to them than
any of the Bayer offerings.

Where did Bayer and its brand managers go wrong with these
consumers?

Presumably, in creating, advertising, and promoting eight distinctive
brand variants, the keepers of Bayer brand believed that they had catered to
every conceivable consumer whim. Taking each of the many marketing tasks
required by each of the eight Bayer brand variants, they must have spent a
great deal of marketing money and professional effort making sure that each
Bayer brand variant got a square marketing shake.

Probably they felt that they had done a good job with each of these individual marketing tasks for each of the Bayer variants. But their satisfaction
with a job well done was based upon the perfection of inconsequential tasks.
The concentration of marketing energy allotted to the Bayer brand was dissi-
pated by this variety of individual activities for each of the Bayer variants.
The result was a fuzzy and contradictory vision of the distinctive satisfaction
that any individual Bayer brand variant might be able to deliver to its
customers.

Without the promise of distinctive consumer satisfaction, a good deal
of marketing's presumed firepower is emasculated: it is hard for advertising
to fulfill its promise; it is difficult for brand loyalty to be built; and it is impossible for the marketer to control the price (and thus the profit) at which
the product or service will be sold.

The end result of the process in the instance that I observed was a lost
customer. Far worse was the loss of the opportunity to create customer satisfaction. If marketing does not provide a basis for creating satisfied customers
for a brand, the long-term vitality of the brand must come into question.

No matter how estimable a brand strategy may seem to be, it fails
when it does not create customer satisfaction. Brand strategy must not
be confused with individual activities such as product development,
advertising, promotion, trade relations, and brand management. All of these

must contribute to the singular conception that is a brand, of course. But the singularity of the brand must precede and direct the execution of all the marketing nuts and bolts.

Creating customer satisfaction is what marketing is supposed to be about. Brand strategy crystallizes the essence of the satisfaction that the brand will offer. If the brand is viewed only as a vehicle to create sales and profits in spite of what consumers want, it is not being marketed — it is simply being sold for a price.

So, to repeat, this is a book about how brand strategies go wrong and how to make them right.

ACKNOWLEDGMENTS

Many people helped me as I wrote this book.

Barbara T. Weilbacher, my daughter, took all the brand photographs that appear in these pages. Besides taking fine pictures, she kept them separate and organized and always knew where the right negative for the ninth variation of a brand or a category was when it was needed.

John Philip Jones and Andrew Ehrenberg read and commented upon particular chapters. They always had wise, important, and helpful things to say, and I am grateful to them for their help.

Bruce Montgomery of Miles Consumer Healthcare Products helped me get permission to reproduce the Alka-Seltzer commercials that appear in the text. This was a thankless task, and I appreciate the time he devoted to it.

Darlene Flaherty, Archivist in the Ford Industrial Arts Archives, helped me develop an understanding of the Taurus/Sable program and all of its implications for brand strategy.

Tracy C. Carlson of CPC International gave me permission to reproduce her wonderful poem about what brand managers really do. I am delighted to have been able to use it.

Ann Knudsen of NTC Business Books worked with me on the manuscript in a thoughtful and professional way and participated in what seemed an endless search for a suitable name for it.

In the end, of course, only I am responsible for the content of the book, for better or for worse. I hope it helps you think about marketing in new ways and makes you a more aggressive and committed brand strategist as a result.

W.M.W.

PART ONE

FIVE MARKETING MYTHS AND THEIR CONSEQUENCES FOR TODAY'S BRAND MARKETERS

Contemporary marketing is based on myths that marketers perceive as realities.

Meanwhile, the corporation organizes and manages itself in a way that insures the perpetuation of these myths.

Chapter 1

Brand Marketing

The goal of marketing in any company has always been to create a small number of very successful and profitable brands. Market leading brands are dependably and bountifully profitable.

Marketing, as it is practiced in the 1990s, can no longer *will* the creation of such dominant, profitable brands. This is in sharp contrast to the powers possessed by at least some marketers as recently as 30 years ago.

In the 1960s, if a company created a better brand—a brand that gave the consumer either more intrinsic value or the illusion of such value, for the same money—sales would follow. The better the consumer perceived the value to be, the greater the sales. The most successful companies of the 1960s—Procter & Gamble; IBM; Anheuser Busch; Sony; American Express; Volkswagen; American Airlines; Pepsico—found ways to deliver more value, either actual or perceived, usually for the same money, sometimes for a slight premium, and occasionally for even less money.

But marketing's ability to develop dominant new brands from scratch is a lost art. In the 1990s, most marketers still go through the marketing motions of the 1960s. But the marketing recipes and formulas of the 1960s do not work in the 1990s: it has become devilishly hard either to give consumers more value or to make consumers believe they are receiving more value.

Nevertheless, the marketing myths of the 1960s prevail. Too many marketers still believe that the only way to gain market dominance is through the continuous development of new brands and brand variants that they hope will become dominant and highly profitable products. New brands and brand variants of products and services continue to flow into the marketplace. But the new brands and brand variants of the 1990s do not have distinction. They are new brands and brand variants of unrelieved sameness.

Simply stated, the old marketing ways do not work anymore. The tragedy is that no new marketing ways have emerged to develop dominant new brands or to resuscitate proud old brands. In this environment most brand sales are made on the basis of equivalent or indistinguishable consumer value. Equal value products are commodities. Commodity products are purchased by consumers on the basis of price, not on the basis of distinguishable product characteristics.

The dilemma of marketing is that it has lost the power to create dominant new brands and brand variants and to control their destiny. Marketing is willing, instead, to make sales at any price.

The cornerstone of marketing is now and has always been, the brand. Brands provide the basis upon which consumers can identify and bond with a product or service or a group of products or services. The brand name assures us that the features and characteristics of the brand will remain invariant from purchase to purchase. In that way, the brand provides its maker with the means to consistently provide the consumer with intrinsic value or the illusion of such value or both.

The idea of brand as value is characterized by such names as Budweiser, United Airlines, Federal Express, Mercedes–Benz, Wheaties, Marlboro, Ford, Smirnoff, Tide, Ivory, Kodak, IBM, Crest, Sony, Maxwell House, Colgate, and on and on. These names represent both the products for which they stand and the warranty that their only purpose is to create continuously a decisive value for consumers.

Marketing creates and manages brands. Successful brands create satisfied customers. Marketing stands or falls on its ability to create satisfied customers.

Chapter 2

What Are the Five Myths of Today's Marketing?

The practice of marketing is hard to get a handle on. There are no universally accepted laws, nor is there a single source of marketing wisdom. Marketers depend on a collection of recipes that have been handed down—mostly verbally—from marketing generation to marketing generation. In a given situation, marketers will use the marketing recipe that they each personally think is most likely to succeed. But across all marketers, there will be no agreement about which recipe is the right one in any given marketing situation.

These recipes become elaborated as time passes. In every company each important new marketing success is more or less considered and more or less absorbed into the recipe-driven marketing doctrine. Well-publicized marketing triumphs of other companies are also studied and absorbed. When young marketers study such past successes, they are led to believe that the past is characterized by accelerating progress. But it is of little good to them, or their companies, if the past is simply repeated mindlessly, with each new "success" merely a smaller scale, desiccated refinement of previous triumphs.

In all of this single-minded emphasis upon past success, or at least what is perceived to be success, postmortem evaluations and analyses of marketing failures are virtually unknown.

Marketing is thus a sort of closed system, feeding upon itself, absorbing and internalizing the successes of the present into the body of doctrine that comes down from the past. Whatever marketing innovations develop within this system are rarely innovations in any absolute sense, but rather only refinements of the past. Past marketing success thus leads to

> ... specialization and exaggeration, to confidence and complacency, to dogma and ritual.[1]

Anyone can have an opinion about marketing. As many young marketers have learned, the marketing opinions of the board chairperson's spouse have their own legitimacy and often seem to be made of sounder currency that those of experienced marketers. Even the marketing heroes of the company must absorb the ideas and theories of their peers into the accumulated wisdom of the company, because this wisdom is not based upon a body of laws or proven theories but upon little more than an accumulation of anecdote and hearsay.

Meanwhile, the academic community studies this process and listens to its practitioners. Instead of standing outside the hurly-burly of marketing and looking in a clear-eyed way at exactly what marketers do and how they might better do what they are supposed to do, the academicians absorb, rationalize, and perpetuate, in the "cases" they prepare for their students, the developed doctrine of marketing practice. In the process, they make marketing past-dependent, sterile, and abstract.

No wonder non-marketing executives have so much trouble trying to understand marketing, and no wonder they have so much difficulty trying to direct it—to make it more responsive to corporate needs and goals and to make its operations more successful and profitable.

As a result of this uncritical agglomeration of the "lessons" of past marketing success, the day-to-day practice of marketing is based upon an interlocking collection of marketing myths. What is now marketing myth was, in 1960, a good deal closer to marketing reality. This reality has gradually transformed itself into myth, comforting marketers that all will be well if they continue to repeat the lessons of the past. But what worked in 1960 will not work now, even though marketers, bemused only with the study and veneration of past successes, believe that it will.

What, in overview, are the five major elements of this mythic marketing doctrine?

MYTH #1 THE CONTINUOUS, FLAMBOYANT DEVELOPMENT OF NEW PRODUCTS INSURES THE FUTURE OF MARKETING

Marketers believe that there is always a new product breakthrough just around the corner. When new product breakthroughs occur, they establish new product categories and new standards of excellence within existing product categories. As new product breakthroughs are absorbed by the market, they will create new customers and a sales momentum of their own, and, thus, so the myth convinces marketers, new products make the system self-perpetuating.

There are at least three ideas that animate the perennial optimism about new products:

- First, is a basic belief in the vast, uncharted promise of technology. A new technological breakthrough seems always to be imminent. The men and women in research and development—aloof, remote, secretive—can be depended upon to bring home the new-product bacon. If there is a single idea that has been ingrained into corporate cultures, it is that meaningful research and development is essential to both near- and far-term corporate well-being.

- A second element that drives the search for new and improved products is the idea of the product life cycle. Every product, so the notion goes, has the kind of experience in life that human beings themselves are heir to. Thus, products are born; nurtured through youth and adolescence; hit their stride in vigorous young adulthood; and then, inevitably, die, as their appeal to consumers—eroded by newer, more modern products—finally passes through a twilight that ends in irrevocable removal from distribution.

  If the successful products of today are inevitably doomed to death, there is every reason to hurry this process along by accelerating the R&D search for improved successors.

- A third force that drives the process of new product development is the idea that markets are fragmented into segments of consumers who have a peculiar set of wants for a particular kind of product within individual product categories.

  This vision of unlimited fragmentation and consequent demand for unlimited brand variations powers the development of myriad brand variations in product category after product category. The

EXHIBIT 2–1   Prepared blue cheese salad dressing brands available in a typical supermarket—1991

premise is that consumers really do have urgently different needs and that brand variants to fulfill these diverse needs will find a receptive market.

In this process, as it is carried through, is the inevitable identification of smaller and smaller segments. This leads to an increasing stream of new brands and brand variants that appeal to fewer and fewer people, as well as being, ultimately, more and more like each other. The end result of this process is illustrated in Exhibit 2–1 for prepared blue cheese salad dressing brands.

Closely aligned to brands that are market segmenters are so-called "line extensions." These are logical elaborations of existing brands. Sometimes it is hard to tell whether new brands are supposed to segment a market or extend an existing brand. Brand variants developed to appeal to specific market segments and/or as line extensions are shown in Exhibit 2–2 for Buick automobiles and in Exhibit 2–3 for Campbell's chicken noodle soup.

1992 BUICK RIVIERA

1992 BUICK PARK AVENUE

1992 BUICK SKYLARK

1992 BUICK ROADMASTER LIMITED

1992 BUICK LESABRE CUSTOM

1992 BUICK REGAL CUSTOM

1992 BUICK CENTURY LIMITED

EXHIBIT 2–2   Buick automobile brand variants designed to segment the automobile market and/or to extend the Buick line—1992

EXHIBIT 2–3   Campbell's chicken noodle soup brand variants designed to segment the chicken soup market and/or to extend the Campbell's soup line–1992

Therefore, marketers believe that the market will *always* absorb new products—technological breakthroughs; replacements for former market leaders that have lost market acceptance and are near death; and products that are carefully crafted to appeal to subsegments within a product market or extend existing brand franchises.

This unrelieved acceptance of the rosy prospects for new products seems rooted in the conviction that consumers can never pass up a new thing. As David Ogilvy, the British advertising man who developed an exceptionally clear-eyed view of the American consumer, said some years ago,

> The two most powerful words you can use in a headline are FREE and NEW. You can seldom use FREE, but you can almost always use NEW —if you try hard enough.[2]

Consumers believe in progress. Progress is all around us. The older we get, the more clearly we can remember the primitive ancestors of current products and the evolution of these primitives into the up-to-date versions that we now enjoy. We *know* that there is an endless stream of new products and we *expect* that among them will be a significant number that will improve in one way or another upon some aspect or aspects of the appeal and performance of those they replace. This embedded anticipation of the new is something that has been around in consumer economies for a long time. It is not something that burst upon American consumers in 1960 or 1970 or 1980.

Susan Strasser remarks on this interactive anticipation between consumers and marketers:

> ... the manufacturers and their marketing consultants have triumphed by creating the cultural definition of progress. At the turn of the century, they offered Americans their version of a society that proceeded from worse to better from bulk goods to packaged ones, from the "dip, dip, dip" of the steel pen to the take-anywhere fountain pen, from the barbershop and the photography studios to the Gillette and the Kodak. Progress would be characterized by an abundance of consumer goods, as up-to-date as tomorrow.[3]

As we shall see in Chapter 3, all of these beliefs about and rationalizations for the importance of new products to marketing have evolved into a preoccupation with new products per se, and a growing indifference to the uniqueness or distinctiveness of these new products.

New product development has become an end in itself. It is driven by two basic forces:

- An obsession with meeting competition

- The incredible capacity of the modern industrial base to turn out an ever-increasing number of variants on a relatively-unchanging number of basic product themes

Marketers in the 1990s are too interested in rushing to market with products that they can say are new, no matter how insignificant the point of difference. After all, new products apparently created many of the great marketing triumphs of the 1950s and 1960s. Secure in the warmth of the myths about new products, contemporary marketers believe that it is just a matter of repeating the new product development and introduction processes that fueled these past triumphs in order to accomplish the same results today.

Unfortunately, as we shall see, this comfortable view of how marketing must work is mostly wrong.

Kenichi Ohmae makes the point:

This heavy investment in competitive differentiation has now gone too far; it has already passed to the point of diminishing returns—too many models, too many gadgets, too many bells and whistles.[4]

MYTH #2 RETAILERS CAN BE USED BY MARKETERS TO ACCOMPLISH MARKETERS' GOALS

Modern retailing has undergone profound changes in the past decade or two —perhaps more profound than any other industry.

For a long time—let us say from 1950 to about 1980—retailers were so concerned about keeping up with their customers that they were virtually forced to let manufacturers have a dominant voice in how they ran their businesses. The marketing programs of the manufacturers had such a powerful hold upon the consumer that retailers were bound to follow the lead of those marketing programs.

And yet at the same time, manufacturers were constrained by the turmoil in retailing as retailers did their best to keep up with consumers who were moving from central city to suburb and becoming more and more affluent.

Marketers often had difficulty achieving widespread distribution of a food or drug product unless that product was distinctive in some way and unless its distinctive features were presold to consumers through advertising. But if a marketer did have such distinctive, presold products, that marketer could virtually force the retail establishment to stock them. It was this set of circumstances that led to the growth of companies—like P&G—that were successful in developing genuinely superior products and had the wit to support them with advertising budgets that would force retailers to stock the products to keep their advertising—conscious customers happy.

Package-goods retailers took a long time to evolve to the point where they could absorb *every* new product that marketers wanted them to stock. The growing importance of retail chains in food, health and beauty aids, and the mass-merchandise categories plus the development of ever-larger retail outlets finally put retailers, by about 1980, in control of their own destiny.

A similar set of circumstances prevailed with consumer durables, as, for example, in home appliances. Franchise agreements insured, in the 1950s, 1960s, and 1970s, that the dealers would dedicate their attention to no more than one or two manufacturers, and the dealers more or less took the merchandise that they were given by the appliance marketers. But this system also had trouble coping with the explosion in population, the explosion in consumer income, and the dispersion of consumers into the suburbs. Ultimately, franchise agreements were scrapped as consumer durable dealers evolved into large-scale, multiline discount operators.

Similarly, automobile retailing gradually evolved from single manufacturer, often single brand, franchisees into multiple manufacturer, multiple line dealers. In addition, auto dealers began to group themselves into auto retailing centers with several unrelated auto dealerships conveniently located adjacent to each other to facilitate consumer shopping.

In the 1980s, package-goods retailers were ready to take decisive control of their businesses. Retailers expanded the size of their stores or dealerships to accommodate all brand comers and strategically located these larger outlets to maximize customer traffic potential.

As this happened, retailers found themselves in a position to impose their will on the marketers rather than the other way round. Stores and dealers are now more than willing to take new brands and new makes and variations and extensions of old brands and old makes. The difference is that the retailers increasingly make the marketer pay for the space that they have available. Marketers either pay for the space itself or they make price concessions to the retailers as they sell their merchandise to them. Meanwhile, these same retailers were also developing their own generic and "house" brands to compete with the other brands on their shelves.

MYTH #3 MARKETERS CONTROL THE PRICES THAT ULTIMATE CONSUMERS PAY FOR THEIR PRODUCTS

Marketers believe that the value of the brands they sell is so distinctive and obvious that they will be able to control the price that consumers pay for their brands. If brands are really distinctive, and if retailers are forced to stock brands because their customers demand that they be made available to them, it is very likely that marketers will be able to set the prices of their brands at a level that yields comfortable and continuing profits.

This happy scenario is no longer what the marketer faces. As brands and brand variants have proliferated and become more and more like each other, and as retailers have been increasingly able to absorb all brand comers, the only way that marketers can induce retailers to stock this plethora of brands and encourage consumers to buy them is through trade promotions and various price concessions of one kind or another.

But it is not only retailers who must be induced to stock brands. Consumers themselves, faced with a steadily increasing flow of ever-more-similar brands and brand variants, are no longer willing to pay a premium price for a brand that is pretty much like its competitors. Because most brands in a product category are now more or less similar, the consumer accordingly makes brand choices on the basis of promotional price reductions in the form of store specials, coupons, promotional offers, factory rebates, and other promotions aimed at the consumer. The marketer can no longer control the prices paid by consumers for the brands that are offered, and, thus, marketing can no longer insulate these brands from price competition, downward fluctuating operating margins, and reduced profits.

MYTH #4 ADVERTISING CAN SOLVE ALL MARKETING PROBLEMS

An enduring marketing myth is that when all other marketing means fail the power of advertising will create brand successes in spite of it.

Marketers believe, or want to believe, that advertising has a unique power to overcome weaknesses in all the other marketing forces. In addition, advertising holds out the promise of achieving very positive marketing results at modest marketing cost. Thus, marketers want to believe that advertising can present new brands and brand variants, distinctive or not, to consumers in beguiling ways.

They also believe that advertising has the ability to build and maintain substantial equity in brand names. Such brand equity will forge, over time, the links of consumer allegiance that guarantee high market shares and profits. This hopeful belief ignores the fact that, in most product categories, brands have been so diluted by brand and brand variant proliferation that there is very little that advertising can realistically do to make most of them truly distinctive. For example, as Exhibit 2–4 suggests, the differentiation of many of the individual brands of bar soaps through advertising is a daunting task.

Marketers want to believe that advertising can continue to force retailers to provide distribution for the advertised products, without significant compensating payments to retailers for the privilege of occupying retail space.

Finally, marketers want to believe that advertising can create consumer perceptions of brand value that make advertised brands impervious to price competition.

No matter what the past successes of advertising, sober marketers of the 1990s have come to conclude that advertising can only rarely accomplish any of these sales-generating tasks. They have also concluded that this is not necessarily because advertising has now become less effective than before, but rather because it can only realize its potential in a marketing environment in which the other myths of marketing are generally true—that distinctive new products can routinely be created; that consumer prices can be controlled by the marketer rather than the retailer; and that marketers can control the distribution of their brands.

MYTH #5 MARKETING ACTIVITIES MAKE CONSUMERS LOYAL TO BRANDS

Marketers believe that marketing can make consumers buy a single brand in a product or service category exclusively; or if consumers do not buy the same brand every time, they will buy it most of the time—perhaps seven purchases out of every ten. If marketing cannot do this, what then is the justification of marketing activity and marketing expenditure?

Marketing is said to create brand loyalty in a number of ways:

- Marketers believe that they can cause brands to be designed that either have or seem to have more value than competitive products at comparable prices. They believe that this shaping of the product offering to make it more desirable to consumers will, when it happens, create brand loyalty.

EXHIBIT 2–4   Brands of bar soap—1992

■ Added to product superiority is the weight of persuasive communication. Advertising creates brand loyalty, so the marketer believes, by making the consumer aware of the substantial benefits offered by the brand. It is this double-barrelled charge—the product of superior value with its promise widely communicated by advertising to those most likely to appreciate it—that epitomizes modern marketing.

■ Even if the product itself is not very different, so the marketing belief goes, its advertising can be made different enough to make the product *seem* different. It is for this reason that some products that appear in every way to be undistinguished from their competitors have been made into dominant brands by the power of advertising alone.

■ Brand loyalty, marketers believe, can also be built through a unique distribution system. And, the better the product with access to a unique distribution channel, the more brand loyalty will be built. If a brand can preempt a distribution channel—as L'eggs pioneered pantyhose distribution through food and drug supermarkets in the early 1970s—brand loyalty is almost certain to result, at least for those consumers who prefer to buy the product in the preempted distribution channel.

■ And brand loyalty can be built by delivering equal or superior quality at a lower price, as Lexus has recently demonstrated in the luxury automobile category.

The lore of marketing insists that real loyalty to brands can and will be built through all of these means. Marketers can *will* consumers to be loyal by offering them better intrinsic value by unique product design; or more psychological or extrinsic value through inspired advertising; or through preemption of a distribution channel; or by the delivery of equal value at a lower price through manufacturing efficiencies or lower margins.

As the evidence in Chapter 7 will reveal, consumers simply do not behave the way marketers believe that they do. Most consumers in 1992 do not become brand loyal most of the time. As a matter of fact, there is a good deal of solid evidence that brand loyalty has never characterized consumer behavior at any time in the past thirty years.

Tod Johnson, president of NPD Research, Inc. (which specializes in consumer-panel-based marketing research and measures continuing consumer brand-purchase behavior) put it this way as early as 1984:

Perhaps the old marketing plans that considered a brand's buyer to be a regular loyal buyer was ... inappropriate, and, thus, the reason that we perceive a brand-loyalty decline now is that marketing management's perception of reality has only gotten closer to the truth.[5]

Brand loyalty makes a good deal of intuitive sense, and is thus ideally suited to its central position in the mythology of marketing. Brand loyal is what consumers *should* become as a result of marketing activities, but in fact consumers do not become loyal, in spite of the onslaught of marketing initiatives. In the end, it is what consumers do that matters, not what marketers think that they do or wish that they would do.

WHAT IS MARKETING ALL ABOUT, ANYWAY?

Marketing to consumers—individuals, families, small businesses, government and nonprofit organizations, giant corporations, whatever—is the art of creating consumer satisfaction. Any product or service or marketing initiative that does not create consumer satisfaction cannot expect to be successful in the long run. Any consumer can be fooled by marketing's wiles once, but few are likely to be fooled twice in a row.

In practice, marketers and marketing tend to fuzz up this basic idea. It gets confused with creating sales to meet quarterly goals, or it evolves into trivial competitive thrusts and parries, or it is confounded by the hubris of manufacturers who believe that what consumers want is incidental to what they, the manufacturers, know how to make. Part of this fuzziness in marketing is due to the strength and pervasiveness of the marketing myths that we have just been talking about. No wonder that brand loyalty is so difficult to create!

Underlying all these myths of marketing is the fact that marketing has come to mean different things to different marketers:

■ In some companies, only too few, marketing means the creation of decisive consumer value—no more, no less.

The idea that marketing should only be concerned with the creation of decisive consumer value is not a new one. Peter Drucker knew what he was talking about in 1954 when he said:

There is only one valid definition of business purpose: *to create a customer* ... Because it is its purpose to create a customer, any business enterprise has two—and only two—basic functions: marketing and innovation.[6]

■ In other companies, marketing means a superficial catering to consumer wants, a preoccupation with razzle-dazzle and puffery at the expense or instead of the creation of decisive consumer value.

One of the most pernicious effects of prior marketing success,
and the myths that it generates, is that marketing itself may deteriorate
into an obsession with the outward trappings of marketing, mistaking
these trappings for the core of customer value that has created the
marketing success in the first place. As Danny Miller points out:

> Unfortunately, salespeople too are subject to a dangerous momen-
> tum that can transform them into unresponsive drifters. They begin
> to substitute packaging, advertising and aggressive distribution for
> good design and competent manufacture. Managers come to believe
> that they can sell anything as they concoct a mushrooming prolifer-
> ation of bland, "me-too" offerings.[7]

The loss of real marketing control leads to a diffusion of effort
and a loss of the final corporate view of what it is that the corporation
must do to make customers.

■ In other companies, usually dominated by engineers, the marketers
come to believe that they know what consumers want better than do
consumers themselves. Such companies arrogantly assume that the
consumer must accept what the company chooses to offer. Such beliefs
and assumptions have long characterized the marketing of automobiles
in the United States. It was only the advent of the German and
Japanese auto imports that has haltingly and imperfectly refocused the
attention of the American automobile manufacturers on their customers and the value those customers demand from the automobiles
they buy and drive.

In those corporations that have lost their fundamental consumer orien-
tation—either because they have substituted the trappings of marketing for
its essence, or because the essence of marketing has dissolved in corporate
arrogance toward the customer—the marketing function cannot focus on the
creation of genuine consumer value. Not much more than lip service is
given to customer needs and satisfactions—the unfocused emphasis is on
marketing razzle-dazzle or manufacturing cost reduction or on the reaching
of sales quotas or all three.

When Pepsico marketing guru, Roger Enrico, was directed by Pepsico
to solve the sales and profit problems of its troubled Frito–Lay subsidiary in
1991, Enrico responded as only a marketing person of the 1980s could or

would. As reported by *Business Week*, Enrico's program does not much involve the consumer:

> [Enrico will] exploit his company's dominance of the market. The cornerstone of this strategy: new products, new sales outlets, new machines.[8]

Marketing myths—new products will be different; distribution can be forced with little or no cost; prices can be set high enough to guarantee generous profits; advertising can overcome other marketing failures; brand loyalty exists—tend to flourish in companies that do not define marketing as the creation of outstanding customer value. In such companies there is a tendency to confuse the process of marketing with the activities of advertising, packaging, selling, and promotion.

In these companies the object of marketing tends to be less consumer driven than competition driven. The key question is not, What does the consumer perceive value to be? but rather, How can I react best to what the competition has just done?

To determine what consumers perceive to be valuable is hard work. It requires the creation of something that is innovative and valuable rather than something that is imitative or merely an iteration—slightly changed—of what competitors have already done.

The key to the solution of the dilemma in marketing is to give marketers the means to *will* the creation of consumer value. It is a topic to which we will turn in the final chapters of this book.

But before we can talk about how marketing *should* be practiced, we must examine the myths of marketing in more detail. In addition we must examine the kinds of adaptive responses that marketers have made as they apply the myths of marketing in ways that exacerbate rather than resolve their marketing problems.

---

[1] The ICARUS PARADOX, copyright © 1990 by Danny Miller, p. 3. Reprinted by permission of HarperBusiness, a division of HarperCollins Publishers, Inc.

[2] Ogilvy, David, *Confessions of an Advertising Man*, Atheneum, New York, 1963, p. 105.

[3] Strasser, Susan, *Satisfaction Guaranteed*, Pantheon Books, New York, 1989, p. 285.

[4] Reprinted by permission of Harvard Business Review. "*Getting Back to Strategy*," by Kenichi Ohmae (November/December 1988), p. 150. Copyright © 1988 by the President and Fellows of Harvard College, all rights reserved.

[5] Johnson, Tod, "The Myth of Declining Brand Loyalty," *Journal of Advertising Research*, 24:1, February–March, 1984, p. 16 .

[6] Drucker, Peter F., *The Practice of Management*, Harper & Brothers, Publishers, New York, 1954, p. 37.

[7] The ICARUS PARADOX, copyright © 1990 by Danny Miller, p. 15. Reprinted by permission of HarperBusiness, a division of HarperCollins Publishers, Inc.

[8] "Chipping Away at Frito–Lay," *Business Week*, July 22, 1991, p. 80.

Chapter 3

Are Distinctive New Products And Services Possible?

Myth #1. The continuous, flamboyant development of new products insures the future of marketing.

We live with the idea of inevitable progress in the quality of our lives. Nowhere is that idea embraced more wholeheartedly than in marketing. Marketers believe that products and services are continually evolving and improving. They also believe that, as products and services evolve and improve, each new product will offer greater value to consumers than did its predecessors.

Once consumers perceive greater product or service value, it is a central dogma of marketing that they will buy the new product in preference to its competitors. Thus, the name of the marketing game is to develop a continuous flow of new products and services that offer consumers greater value. If the idea of progress is foreordained, then the idea of newer, better products is its handmaiden.

The idea of product and service progress has led, inevitably, to brand and brand-variant proliferation. In category after category, the number of products and services that the consumer could choose from multiplied in the 1970s and remultiplied in the 1980s. A walk through the aisles of a supermarket, or into an automobile dealership, or into a consumer electronics store provides stunning testimony to American ingenuity, technological ubiquity, and a fundamental dedication to new brands and new variations in old brands.

The only marketing justification for a new product or service is that it will make the life of those who buy it better in some way—easier, more pleasurable, more rewarding, or more affordable—and, thus, be more valuable to its purchaser than competitive products.

Of course, from the standpoint of marketing, the more the product or service is changed and improved and, thus, embodies greater value, the better will be its user's way of life. The more positive and identifiable the change, the greater the prospect of sales.

One of the truisms of marketing is, of course, that many new products fail. Philip Kotler, citing a study of the Conference Board, reports that:

... The new product failure rate was 40 percent for consumer products, 20 percent for industrial products, and 18 percent for services.[1]

It is not at all clear exactly what statistics of this kind mean. A new product or service may be a genuine innovation or a refinement or a market segmenter, or merely a line extension. Genuine innovations that are meaningful and economic for consumers do not often fail. But there *are* many failures among product or service variations that are trivial or imitative of other products.

Another way to think about this is that the enhanced value offered by many, if not most, new products or services just does not appeal to consumers very much. Perhaps the increment in value offered is too small for consumers to care about.

The heart of marketing lies here. It is the job of the marketer to define and design new products and services that consumers will want. To say that 40 percent or 20 percent or 18 percent—or whatever percent—of new products fail is to say that marketers are not very good at finding new products that promise an increment in value that is decisive to consumers.

Yet the reality is that the retail stores and dealerships abound in brand diversity and brand variation. If one wished to purchase an expensive automobile in 1992—one, for example, that cost more than $25,000, there were 57 individual brand models to choose from, as shown in Exhibit 3–1. Each of these brand models may also have one or more engine power or accessory options packages available. And if one wants to buy coffee, the typical store may offer 10 or 12 or more different brands of coffee to choose from, as shown in Exhibit 3–2. Again, most of these different brands also have, in addition, one or more variations in brew or flavor or formulation to choose from.

Although a lot of new products do fail in any year, it is true that at least some do survive. The cumulative effect of such survivals has been to produce a massive proliferation of brands and brand variants in product and service category after product and service category.

Every one of these new brands and brand variants was designed, presumably, to offer the consumer some sort of greater value than that offered by competitive brands. Every one of these new brands and brand variants was designed, presumably, to change the quality of life enough to appeal at least to some consumers, and the more the better.

TECHNOLOGY AS A SOURCE OF NEW PRODUCTS AND SERVICES

New products and services and their new brands and brand variants come about for a variety of reasons: by far the most important is the promise of new technology. Technology, properly applied and extended, will lead to a smooth flow of new products and services. New products and services come about because, in most companies, there is a conscious effort, if not an obsession, to develop and perfect them.

Marketers, believing that progress is inevitable, do their best to make sure that it characterizes their own products and services. The research and development budget almost guarantees that this obsession with product/service improvement and progress will become a self-fulfilling prophecy. There will be technological innovations in products and services because manufacturers budget to make sure that technological innovation occurs.

The truth of the matter is, of course, that there are technological innovations and there are technological innovations. One can think of a continuum of technological developments that range from the mundane brand extension, to the modest brand refinement, to the genuinely new product or service.

There are few really genuine new products or services in any one year or, for that matter, in any one decade. In recent years such genuine innovations in consumer products or services have tended to come in those areas where the bulk of technological exploration has focused— either because of military need or because of perceived economic opportunity or both.

Thus, genuine new product breakthroughs have been most likely to come in fields such as consumer electronics or pharmaceuticals. The quality of our lives has thus been improved by personal computers; compact discs and disc players; video cassettes and video cassette players; by an accelerated flow of new pharmaceutical preparations—first as prescription drugs and later as drugs switched from prescription to over-the-counter status.

Brand Models	List Price
Infiniti M30 6 Cpe	$ 25,000
Lexus ES300 6	25,250
Audi 80 Quattro 5	26,250
Acura Legend (Base Car) 6	27,450
Audi 100 6	27,700
Mazda 929 6	27,800
BMW 325i 6	27,990
SAAB 9000S 4	28,095
BMW 318 IC 4 Convert	28,870
Mercedes 190E 4	28,950
Acura Legend L 6	29,850
Audi 100S 6	29,900
SAAB 9000CD 4	30,195
Lexus SC300 6 Cpe	31,100
Acura Legend L 6 Cpe	31,300
Lincoln Cont Exec 6	32,263
Audi 100CS 6	32,900
Mercedes 190E 6	34,000
Lincoln Cont Sig 6	34,253
Acura Legend LS 6	34,350
Cadillac Seville 8	34,975
BMW 525i 6	35,600
Acura Legend LS 6 Cpe	35,700
SAAB 9000 Turbo 4	36,045
BMW 3251 C Convert	36,320
SAAB 9000CD Turbo 4	36,695
Lexus SC400 8 Cpe	37,500
Cadillac Seville Touring 8	37,975
Infiniti Q45 8	42,000
SAAB 9000 Griffin 4	42,195
Lexus LS400 8	42,200
Mercedes 300D 5	42,950
Mercedes 300E 2.6	42,950
BMW 535i 6	44,350
Jaguar XJ6 6	44,500
Jaguar Sovereign 6	49,500
Mercedes 300E	49,500
BMW 735i 6	52,990
Mercedes 300TE Wagon	53,900

EXHIBIT 3–1   Automobiles costing more than $25,000 in America and their list prices—1992

(Continued)

Jaguar Vanden Plas 6	54,500
Mercedes 400E 8	55,800
BMW 735iL 6	56,950
Mercedes 300E 4 Matic	57,100
Jaguar Vanden Plas MAJ 6	59,500
Mercedes 300CE Cpe	60,400
Jaguar XJ12 12 Cpe	60,500
Mercedes 300TE 4 Matic	61,100
Acura NSX	63,000
Jaguar XJ12 12 Convert	67,500
Mercedes 300SD 6	69,400
Mercedes 300SE 6	69,400
Mercedes 400SE 8	77,900
Mercedes 500E 8	79,200
Mercedes 300SL 6 Cpe	82,500
Mercedes 500SEL 8	93,500
Mercedes 500SL 8 Cpe	97,500
Mercedes 600SEL 12	127,800

And businesses, large and small, have become fundamentally more efficient and productive as a result of the development of the telephone answering device and the facsimile (fax) machine.

These are products that have come into being where no other comparable product has previously existed. When such products are first presented to consumers as brands, the brand name often comes to symbolize the product category itself, as in the case of Kodak, Frigidaire, Coke, Cellophane, Kleenex, Xerox, and so forth.

Marketers tend to be leery of introducing genuine product or service innovations that are new but not of obvious import to the consumer. They shy away from such products because, as pointed out above, such marginal innovations often fail. But marketers also shy away from such innovative new products because the cost of introducing them is very high. H. John Greeniaus, president of Nabisco Brands, Inc., makes the point:

> Creating new brands is unbelievably expensive. There are no hard statistics on this subject, but I'm sure all of you would agree that it's impossible to introduce a genuinely new consumer package goods brand for less than $20 million, and doing it right probably costs $50 million or more.[2]

In the middle range of the continuum of technological innovations are brand refinements—sometimes quite dramatic refinements based upon

EXHIBIT 3–2   Coffee brands available in a typical supermarket—1992

previously existing technology. Existing brands absorb the refinements that are developed by technologies narrowly focused upon the improvement of what already exists.

Thus, for example, the fax machines are combined with telephone answering devices; air conditioners and hot water heaters appear with double the efficiency of their predecessors; existing cereals are modified with the addition of sugar or other sweeteners; premium coffee brands appear in new blends, roasts, and grinds as the handling, sorting, and processing of coffee beans is developed and refined.

These refinements may represent genuine improvements to be sure, but they are refinements of existing product types, rather than genuinely new products. Such refinements can often be used—at least until the competitors catch up—to differentiate brands.

Finally, there are changes in brands that represent modest improvements at best, if they be improvements at all. These brands represent relatively slight variations over their competitors. They are based on product differences that may be made to seem real and better but are neither genuine nor important refinements.

The important characteristic of this final class of new products is that their differences from their predecessors and competitors are usually not self-evident. Rather, these trivial differences must be drawn to the attention of and explained to the consumer if they are to be made at all meaningful. It is at this level of product development that brand offerings especially tend to proliferate, usually in an attempt to gain some minimum competitive advantage, to match a competitive thrust, or to present the consumer with a more complete range of brand offerings.

One can think, in this connection, of a communications continuum that shadows the product-innovation continuum. In the case of genuine product or service innovations, all that the consumer who will want to use such products needs to know is that the new product or service exists—its benefits speak for themselves and are self-evident, as in the case of the first consumer-friendly snapshot camera or mass produced refrigerator or the Federal Express system of overnight package delivery. A straightforward statement of the facts of the product is all the communication that is needed to inform or intrigue consumers about such product innovations. The brand names need only be made synonymous with the innovation.

In the case of product refinements, more extensive and informative communication is required. The exact nature of the product refinement must be revealed, as well as the import of this refinement for the consumer.

The virtues of four-wheel drive or of the anti-lock braking system are not, at least to the uninitiated consumer, self-evident. The evidence of fuel efficiency in air conditioners and water heaters must be presented and explained, and the implications of this improved efficiency must be demonstrated.

Communications about brand refinements must start from the level of performance of the unrefined brand and show to what extent and with what implication this existing level of performance has been exceeded. The meaning and import of such brand refinement must be continuously reinforced as other brands develop comparable, if not identical, refinements.

Finally, there are the communications needs of brand innovations that are neither genuine innovations nor serious refinements of existing brands. It is necessary, in the case of such brand modifications, for communications about them to make them *seem* different enough to interest consumers. The communications must assert this difference, imply its superiority, and, finally, make up for the fact that the brand variant itself is neither very much different or at all better than its predecessors and competitors.

Of course, it is this latter group of brands—those that are differentiated not by intrinsic product characteristics but rather by the extrinsic assertions of communication—that make up a large portion of today's new brands. It is difficult, if not impossible, for manufacturers to develop, even through accelerated and enhanced research and development, a continuous flow of either innovative or really refined new products. Despite this, the demands of product and service "progress" itself must be satisfied, and the expense of research and development must be justified. So the consumer must settle for brands and brand variants that are really not much different from their predecessors and competitors but can be made to seem at least somewhat different through communication.

This phenomenon—we may call it communication-inspired innovation —is not something that has developed only in the last decade or two. A classic example involves the marketing of the Gillette "blue blade" in the mid-1930s. The "blue blade" was apparently an acceptable shaving implement, but it represented neither a genuine product improvement nor a significant product refinement. What it was, in fact, was a perfectly good razor blade that was colored blue *to make it seem different.*

Gerard Lambert, then president of the Gillette Company, has recounted the tale:

When I knew we had a much better blade, the sharpest in the country, I asked one of the engineers to join me at lunch at the restaurant in the South Station [in Boston], where we generally ate. After lunch, I asked him if he could color a blade blue. Certainly, he could do it. He would put on a blue lacquer. I made it clear to him that I did not want a blade to look like blue steel. I just wanted a different color, something other than plain steel.[3]

The important point for Mr. Lambert appears to have been not that he had an intrinsically better blade but that he had made it *appear* to be a better blade by imparting a blue color to it.

THE PRODUCT LIFE CYCLE

Another fundamental belief about products is that, just as new products will (must) be created, old products will inevitably wither and die. This is the notion of the *product life cycle*, wherein every product is an anthropomorphic analog of life itself: it is born; it gradually moves toward maturity; it begins to decline in consumer favor; and it finally dies because most consumers do not want it anymore. The inevitable death of old products creates, therefore, a continuing need for new products.

Many marketing thinkers are quite adamant about the strength of the product life-cycle concept and its implications for marketing practice. For example, Philip Kotler has written, in a passage that could easily have come from any of the leading marketing textbooks:

No branded product can be expected to hold a permanent franchise in the marketplace. The lifetime sales of many products reveal a typical pattern of development. This pattern is known as the *product life cycle*.[4]

There is an obvious inconsistency in this line of thought: products are not the same as brands. Products—automobiles, toothpastes, CD players, whatever—are subject to the processes of innovation and refinement that we have just sketched out. A product will survive as long as it is not replaced by a totally new kind of product—CDs replace black vinyl discs, ready-to-eat cereals replace hot cereals, etc. The life of a distinct product can, indeed, be described in life-cycle terms.

Brands, on the other hand, are the very essence of marketing. A brand is a proprietary version of a product. A brand must somehow be differentiated from its competition to survive. If there is a *brand* life cycle, it is a reflection of the strengths and weaknesses of the marketing efforts that are brought to bear upon the brand. Brands may have an articulated life cycle that ends in their death, but if they do, it is because they have not been managed or marketed as well as they should have been and not because it is inevitable that they will die.

There are lots of examples of branded products whose robust sales after many decades of marketplace presence belie the whole notion of the brand life cycle: Gold Medal Kitchen Tested Flour; Lipton Tea; Campbell Soup; Coca–Cola; Kodak; Shell Gasoline; Colgate Toothpaste; Wrigley Chewing Gum; Gillette Razors; Ivory Soap; Sherwin–Williams Paint; Hershey Chocolate Bars; Ford Automobiles. All of these brands should have long since passed into the limbo of life-cycle death if the basic notion of the brand life cycle is valid. So it does not follow that brands must inevitably die.

If the intrinsic product is superannuated by an innovative new product —buggies replaced by automobiles—it is up to the managers of the buggy brands to develop a strategy to absorb the new technology. This may not be as easy as it sounds. Of all the buggy makers who might have gone into the automobile business, only one—Studebaker—survived long enough to tell the tale, and the Studebaker Company was ultimately unable to compete successfully in the automobile marketplace. It produced its last automobile in the early 1950s.

Of course, the manufacturer and the manufacturer's marketers may dominate the technology in a product category for a long time—always maintaining a technological advantage by replacing existing products with innovative new products—thus managing the life cycle of successive products.

For example, the technology underlying shaving of male facial hair has been transformed in a series of product innovations by the Gillette Company since King C. Gillette first conceived of the disposable razor blade around 1900. Disposable razor blades became steel blades which, in turn, became "blue blades"; then, stainless steel blades; then, movable strip blades; then, double angled blades; then, double flexible angled blades; then, double flexible blades with plastic strip to increase shave smoothness; then, the double "sensor" blades.

Who can tell what the next Gillette innovation in male facial shaving will be?

Note the difference between Studebaker and Gillette. Studebaker managers absorbed the automobile technology as automobiles replaced buggies. However, they were not able to dominate the evolution of automobile technology sufficiently well to remain competitive in the automobile market. Thus, the company withered and died.

Gillette, however, has dominated the technology of facial shaving by males for at least the last 90 years. No other company has succeeded in marketing an innovative new shaving product in competition with Gillette during this time period. The Gillette marketing performance has, indeed, been superior.

Even if the technological innovations are not homegrown, it is important for the manufacturer to be alert for new product innovations that may extend or replace the basic technology that now serves a particular consumer need. The genuine technological innovation by an upstart tinkerer or inventor is too often perceived not as the work of a potential friend or business partner but as the product of a mortal enemy. In such instances, it is better to attempt to absorb the enemy than to wage a war that, ultimately, cannot be won.

Marketing is concerned with the future of the brand in an innovative environment. Marketing is concerned with the survival of the brand as technology evolves. If the company cannot perpetuate a technological dominance in a product category, the brand as such must fail.

In the case of products that are subject to continuing refinement, such as automobiles, powdered soaps and detergents, coffees, etc., etc., it is up to marketing to identify the refinements that will survive in the marketplace and to manage the brands in terms of those refinements. In the case of those products that are or appear to be beyond meaningful refinement—breakfast foods, candy, soft drinks, and all the others—it is up to marketing to manage the development of minor brand refinements or communications-based brand variants that will achieve some acceptance in the marketplace.

The idea of the product life cycle for brands in the marketplace is, setting aside the revolutionary product innovation, completely an issue of marketing competence. It is an issue of identifying meaningful brand refinements and preempting them for the brand. It is an issue of identifying viable communications-based product variants and preempting them for the brand.

The practice of marketing, in this sense, is inevitably, as brands and brand variants proliferate and become more and more alike, a challenge of making more and more out of less and less.

MARKET SEGMENTATION

Another source of pressure for product differentiation lies in the idea that most, if not all, markets are segmented. This means that different consumers prefer different product or brand variations. Some consumers prefer toothpastes that will make their teeth white (Aim); others prefer fluoridated toothpastes (Crest); others prefer toothpastes that will make their breath fresh (Close-Up); and yet others prefer toothpastes that combine two or

EXHIBIT 3–3   Toothpaste brands available in a typical supermarket—1991

more of these attributes (Aqua-fresh). The wide variety of segmented products in the toothpaste category is suggested in Exhibit 3–3.

An alternative meaning for marketing segmentation is that there are groups of people with like beliefs or lifestyles who prefer particular products because they are perceived to be positively related to these consumers' visions of themselves. Thus, Pepsi–Cola is for the "Pepsi generation."

In segmented marketing the opportunity for the marketer is defined by the number of product or personality segments that the marketer can identify for the product category of the brand being managed. The energy of product refinement is now harnessed to those consumption segments that depend upon consumer preferences for alternative product characteristics.

As Norman Barnett points out:

> ... The process of segmentation becomes the search for new, and as yet nonexistent, combinations of product characteristics for which there is significant unmet consumer demand.[5]

Similarly, the energy of communication-based product differentiation must now be harnessed to alternative-communications strategies that create either product-based or personality-based product differences that will appeal to the market segments that they have been created to exploit.

The marketer's task is to find segments that can be exploited either by product/brand variations or by ideas about product/brand variations.

The idea of segmentation is certainly not a new one. The creation of products that are differentiated by end use has been practiced by craftspeople and manufacturers for centuries. Thus, for example, as George Basalla reports, an American axe maker in 1863 produced 13 different kinds of hand axes, each to be used in presumably a different task or setting. The individual axes bore such names as "Kentucky," "Ohio," "Yankee," "Maine," "Michigan," "Jersey," "Georgia," "North Carolina," "Turpentine," "Spanish," "Doublebilled," "Fire Engine," and "Boy's-handled." By 1898, the same manufacturer offered more than 100 different brands of hand axes.[6]

And, in an insight that crops up repeatedly in the marketing literature, Alfred P. Sloan of the General Motors Corporation decreed that his company would not make a single, universal automobile as did his competitor, Ford, but would instead make a line of automobiles: "A car for every purse and purpose."[7]

Thus was born the General Motors line of automobiles: Cadillac, LaSalle, Oldsmobile, Buick, Pontiac, Chevrolet, and Saturn.

The notion of segmentation leads, inevitably, to brand proliferation and, through normal competition, to the proliferation of brand variants.

It is one thing to identify a meaningful segment—different auto-mobiles for different income levels; different axes for different usage situations; toothpastes with different end benefits; etc. It is another thing to create a brand for a segment that is only weakly differentiated from other segments: for segments that only exist in the imagination of the marketer; or for segments that come about only because of a manufacturing capability, not consumer demand or desire. Whenever a product is created for a weak or nonexistent segment, meaningless brand and brand variant proliferation occurs.

The real trick in successful market segmentation is to create a product category that will cause consumers to switch to it more or less permanently. As competitive brands then proliferate, consumers may switch their allegiances among them, but they will always buy only brands created for this particular segment. Successful segmented marketing means the calculated creation of brands that are not merely acceptable substitutes for products that already exist.

By this standard, many market segments are really not very meaning-ful. For example, Exhibit 3–4 shows brand variants in the coffee category that are, presumably, designed to segment the market. Note that each of the coffee brands shown previously in Exhibit 3–2 may be segmented in three or four different ways as shown in Exhibit 3–4; thus, a multiplier effect occurs as each brand is proliferated to meet each of the segmenters devel-oped by other brands. Toothpaste brands may also multiply through appar-ent segmentations of the market. Exhibit 3–5 shows 13 Crest brand variants. Some of these may segment the toothpaste market in a meaningful way.

Marketers have too long emphasized the search for new segments. Consumers have long been mostly indifferent to this search. They perceive products within categories—whatever grammar of segmentation the mar-keters have imposed upon the product category—as being mostly inter-changeable. Consumers simply do not always keep their purchases within the product segments as the theory of market segmentation suggests they should—they routinely buy across segments, as we shall see in Chapter 7.

LINE EXTENSIONS AS A SOURCE OF NEW PRODUCTS

Another way in which new products come about is through the "extension" of an existing brand. New variants of the brand are created which, in one way or another, are logically related to the basic brand. Sometimes such line extensions are developed to appeal to specific market segments. In the case of the coffee brands and Crest toothpaste shown in Exhibits 3–4 and 3–5,

EXHIBIT 3–4 Coffee brand variants designed to segment the coffee market and/or extend individual brand lines—1991

EXHIBIT 3–5   Crest brand variants designed to segment the toothpaste
market and/or extend the Crest line—1991

it is impossible to tell whether the variants were originally intended to segment or extend the markets.

In other instances, the line extension is simply designed to extend the appeal of the basic brand, although no specific consumer segment has been identified as a target for the line extension. In such instances, the appeal of the line extension may be to existing customers—a "cannibal" extension—or to current nonusers of the brand.

Take, for example, the Oreo brand of cookies. The traditional Oreo—a chocolate "sandwich" cookie with a white creme filling—has been extended in a variety of ways as illustrated in Exhibit 3–6.

H. John Greeniaus characterizes such extensions of the Oreo brand as a stretch of brand equity. Greeniaus outlines the intrinsic-product ground rules under which extensions of the Oreo line will be permitted to occur, as follows:

... We allow ourselves to alter the size of the cookie as long as it is round.

We can vary the amount of creme in the center.

We can change the color of the creme as long as it tastes the same.

We can use different outside coatings for the cookie.

And, finally, we can play with the size and shape of the package as long as the trademark is consistent.[8]

Greeniaus also outlines the extrinsic or communication-based characteristics of Oreo that guide the extension of communications about the brand:

... We have a very clear and comprehensive understanding of the brand's consumer image. Oreo is fun and playful; it is never serious or somber. Oreo is irresistably delicious. Oreo is part of living. It is as American as apple pie. Oreo is loved by the whole family. It is truly for the kid in all of us, which encompasses all age groups. And Oreo evokes rich associations of family, friends, youth, and indulgence.[9]

The basic fact is that brands and brand variants proliferate—sometimes in the name of market segmentation; sometimes in the name of line extension; sometimes, so it would seem, with no reasonable rationale at all. It becomes proliferation for the sake of proliferation. Whatever the rationale for proliferation, it produces a powerful multiplier of individual brand

EXHIBIT 3–6   Oreo brand extensions—1991

entities, as the coffee variants in Exhibit 3–4 and the Crest variants in Exhibit 3–5 attest.

STAGNANT CONSUMER MARKETS

Marketers know, or should know, that as they proliferate brands through refinement, market segmentation, and line extension, all the new entities must be absorbed by product markets that are in themselves not growing very rapidly, if at all. Aside from volume growth due to small increases in the population from year to year, established consumer markets are essentially stagnant. True, there is substantial growth in markets created by genuine product innovations, as in the case in recent years of personal computers and CD players and records. But markets whose sales are not fueled by genuine innovation grow hardly at all.

John Philip Jones makes the point:

This lack of market vitality appears irreversible since it represents a seemingly permanent ceiling on consumers' purchase levels in all except a few areas—mainly financial and other services and high tech, not the traditional categories of packaged goods and consumer durables.[10]

If most consumer goods markets are stagnant, a proliferation in the number of brands that compete in these markets means, of course, that as new brands and brand variants emerge, the share expectation of any individual brand or brand variant in the market, including the new ones, must diminish.

A NEGATIVE ANSWER TO A QUESTION

In the title of this chapter we asked the question, "Are distinctive new brands possible?" The answer to this question, on the evidence of contemporary marketing accomplishment, seems to be, at best, only occasionally.

As we have seen, technology institutionalized as research and development has become an end in itself, looking always for the genuine product innovation, often settling for a more or less meaningful product refinement, usually contenting itself with product differences that can only be exploited by what the manufacturer communicates about the product rather than by what the product is. Brand refinement, segmentation, and line extension must, as they proliferate, inevitably lead to smaller and smaller differences between brands and brand variants and their competitors as well as to smaller and smaller market shares for each.

Business Week magazine has featured, in recent years, a compilation of what its editors believe to be the "best" new products of the preceding year. We take this as an earnest and well-researched endeavor to illustrate contemporary standards of new product development. If there have been genuine product innovations in a given year, certainly they will be found in this selection. If such product innovations are not to be found in this list, and if, in fact, the list is dominated by brand refinements, market segmenters, and line extensions, this can only reflect the current state of product development and, especially, the low level of genuine product innovation.

When we look at the 38 "best new products of the year" as identified by the editors of *Business Week* for 1989 (Exhibit 3–7), 1990 (Exhibit 3–8), and 1991 (Exhibit 3–9), only three can be described as genuine product innovations, 22 can be described as brand refinements, and 13 seem to be either market segmenters or brand extensions.

One innovation, found on the 1989 list, is the Black & Decker Steam Works, a wallpaper stripping machine. A second innovation, found on the 1991 list, is a new prescription drug—Ceredase—that will stop and reverse Gaucher's disease. The third innovation, also on the 1991 list, is a Tandy computer that accepts hand-printed words as input.

THE BEST NEW PRODUCTS OF 1989

1. Sun Microsystems RISC computation system	Refinement
2. Reebok inflatable air shoe	Refinement
3. Campbell Soup 'N Sandwich microwave combo	Extension
4. Black & Decker Steam Works wallpaper removal machine	Innovation
5. Motorola Ultraslim Microtrack portable cellular phone	Refinement
6. Toyota Lexus	Refinement
7. Sportscope sporting event periscope	Refinement
8. Sony Microcom camcorder	Refinement
9. Compaq LTE laptop computer	Refinement
10. Chevrolet Corvette ZR–1	Extension
11. Zelco Thumper fumble free alarm clock	Extension
12. Samsonite Piggy Back Silhouette 4 suitcase/luggage cart	Refinement

Source: *Business Week*, January 8, 1990, pp. 127–29. Used by special permission. Copyright by McGraw Hill, Inc.

EXHIBIT 3–7   *Business Week* "best new products"—1989

THE BEST NEW PRODUCTS OF 1990

1. Gillette "sensor" razor	Refinement
2. IBM RS/6000 workstation	Refinement
3. Burger King Broiled-Not-Fried chicken	Extension
4. Honda Acura NSX	Extension
5. AT&T Universal card	Refinement
6. Cross mountain bike	Extension
7. Main Street Toy Slap Wraps	Refinement
8. Cadet Manufacturing Encore Wave thermometer	Refinement
9. Ford Explorer	Extension
10. Fisher–Price infant car seat	Refinement
11. Mitsubishi PRIMI VCR tuner	Refinement
12. Microsoft Window 3.0 computer program	Refinement

Source: *Business Week*, January 14, 1991, pp. 124–26. Used by special permission. Copyright by McGraw Hill, Inc.

EXHIBIT 3–8   *Business Week* "best new products" — 1990

THE BEST NEW PRODUCTS OF 1991

1. Compton's Multi-Media Encyclopedia CD-ROM	Extension
2. Cadillac Seville Touring Sedan	Refinement
3. Genzyme Ceredase enzyme enhancer	Innovation
4. Hewlett–Packard Palmtop computer	Segmenter
5. Nabisco Brands Mini Oreos	Extension
6. Tandy Grid Pad computer	Innovation
7. Crown Equipment four-wheel counter-balanced setdown forklift	Refinement
8. Trimble Navigation Trimpak global positioning system	Extension
9. Chrysler Minivan children's car seat	Refinement
10. Dodge Viper	Refinement
11. Woodzig power pruner	Refinement
12. Eastern Sports Ultralight baseball bat	Segmenter
13. Sierra Club/Earthwatch Ecovacations	Segmenter
14. Apple PowerBook computer	Refinement

Source: *Business Week*, January 13, 1992, pp. 123–27. Used by special permission. Copyright by McGraw Hill, Inc.

EXHIBIT 3–9   *Business Week* "best new products" — 1991

Note well that these collections of new products are not random selections. They have been carefully chosen to represent the best and most innovative new products in 1989, 1990, and 1991.

If these "new" products are not, in general, especially distinctive or innovative, the question remains: What *can* be done to create distinctive new products? And this immediately leads to another question: If distinctive new products are possible at all, are they most likely to come about through technological means or through marketing means?

In the first place, if the history of technology teaches us nothing else, it teaches that innovation is inevitable. There will be important consumer product innovations in the future, and they will create distinctive new products and distinctive new product categories. But this is just about all that we can be certain about.

No one knows how many important and genuine consumer product innovations will occur in the foreseeable future or at any given point in that future. No one knows what these innovations will be. No one knows which of the existing and entrenched consumer product categories will be destroyed by the still unknown but inevitable innovations.

There is strong evidence, however, that it is difficult to force the pace of innovation. As Root–Bernstein observes:

> The American Chemical Society made a list of the most significant advances in chemistry–pure and applied–a few years ago, and two photography journals have likewise evaluated the history of breakthroughs in photography. All three of these studies show the same thing. Over as much as a hundred and fifty years, there has been no increase in the rate of discovery, despite a several-hundredfold increase in the number of investigators in each field....
>
> Most striking is recent evidence that the number of patents being filed by U.S. citizens has been declining over the last few decades.[11]

The pace of innovation, it would seem, does not correlate very impressively with the number of people or the amount of money or resources that are dedicated to it. So, there is little consolation in the fact that the number of scientists and engineers employed by industry in research and development work has increased by 58 percent between 1970 and 1987, nor in the fact that industry committed 94 percent more (constant) dollars to research and development in 1987 than in 1970.[12]

Even if R&D efforts continue to grow, the number of genuine innovations that they are likely to produce will probably not increase much from year to year.

If there is to be reform in the product development process, this reform must certainly come from marketing rather than from technology. This is a challenge that most marketers are glad to accept. The instinct of the successful marketer is to plunge forward—either with R&D's help or not—in perpetual pursuit of inevitable progress: in products, brands, and brand variants, ever ignoring the litter of undifferentiated, old-"new" products that this instinct has produced in the past.

Philip Kotler has described these remains of the marketing process as it is now practiced:

> Executive conversation is rich with talk of "sick" products, "slow movers," "superannuated" products, "senior citizens," "parasites," "former heavyweights," "obsolete lines," and "fizzled out" products. All kinds of products are involved, including those which never quite got off the ground, those whose profit returns were fair for a while and are now vanishing, and those which were huge successes and are now riding in a sea of troubles.[13]

The real issue is what can marketing do to discipline this process of marginal brand differentiation and brand proliferation. This is a question that will be addressed in some detail in the second section of this book.

The key to reform in marketing is discipline in marketing. Fueled by the boundless optimism of the sales mentality and fed by an unquestioning belief in the inevitability of progress, the practice of marketing has simply gotten out of hand.

It has gotten out of hand because marketers believe, correctly, that it is their responsibility continuously to improve the flow of new and improved products and services to consumers. This is the work of marketing. The success of marketing is measured by the marketers' ability to do this.

The problem is that there are simply not that many new products and services that are more valuable to consumers than the products and services that are currently available to them. Marketing has failed to find a way to institutionalize and regularize the development of new products and services that have decisive consumer value.

In the absence of new products and services of decisive consumer value, marketing has settled for their surrogates—brand refinements, brand segmenters, and brand extenders. As the full force of competition comes into play, these surrogates develop a powerful multiplier effect—the number of brands and brand variants explodes. Since these surrogates for products and services of decisive consumer value are more or less like each other, the consumer derives little or no new value from the process.

It is only recently that the retail system has evolved to a point where it can absorb all these brand refinements, segmenters, and extenders. In fact, had this evolution in retailing not taken place, there would have been no retail place for all these brands and brand variants to go. It is to this evolution of the retail system that we turn in Chapter 4.

---

[1] Kotler, Philip, *Marketing Management*, Sixth Edition, Prentice Hall, Englewood Cliffs, N. J., 1988, p. 407.

[2] Greeniaus, H. John, "Getting the Organization to Think Brand Power," *81st Annual Meeting and Business Conference Showcase*, Association of National Advertisers, Inc., New York, 1990, p. 140.

[3] Lambert, Gerard, *All Out of Step*, Doubleday & Company, Inc., Garden City, N. Y., 1956, p. 188.

[4] Reprinted by permission of *Harvard Business Review*. "Phasing Out Weak Products," by Philip Kotler (March/April, 1965), p. 108. Copyright © 1965 by the President and Fellows of Harvard College, all rights reserved.

[5] Reprinted by permission of *Harvard Business Review*. "Beyond Market Segmentation," by Norman L. Barnett (January/February, 1969), p. 162. Copyright © 1969 by the President and Fellows of Harvard College, all rights reserved.

[6] Basalla, George, *The Evolution of Technology*, Cambridge University Press, Cambridge, 1988, p. 89.

[7] Sloan, Alfred P., *My Years With General Motors*, Doubleday & Company, Inc., Garden City, N. Y., 1964, p. 67.

[8] Greeniaus, H. John, "Getting the Organization to Think Brand Power," *81st Annual Meeting and Business Conference Showcase*, Association of National Advertisers, Inc., New York, 1990, p. 144.

[9] Ibid., p. 144.

[10] Reprinted by permission of *Harvard Business Review*. "The Double Jeopardy of Sales Promotions," by John Philip Jones (September/October, 1990), p. 145. Copyright © 1990 by the President and Fellows of Harvard College, all rights reserved.

[11] Root–Bernstein, Robert Scott, *Discovering*, Harvard University Press, Cambridge, 1989, pp. 39–40.

[12] *Statistical Abstract of the United States, 1990*, U. S. Department of Commerce, Bureau of the Census, Washington, 1990, Tables 997, 985.

[13] Reprinted by permission of *Harvard Business Review*. "Phasing Out Weak Products," by Philip Kotler (March/April, 1965), p. 109. Copyright © 1965 by the President and Fellows of Harvard College, all rights reserved.

Chapter 4

Brand Proliferation and the Retailing System

Myth #2. Retailers can be used by marketers to accomplish marketers' goals.

In the 1930s most people bought most things with the help of a clerk. The concept of self-service was virtually unknown.

When, for example, someone shopped for groceries, it was almost always in a long narrow store with floor to ceiling shelves lining the walls and a stark counter along one side. Behind the counter stood grocery clerks.

The shopper told a clerk, when one became available, the items to be purchased. He—the clerks were inevitably male—fetched each item as the shopper asked for it, one by one, either from the shelves or from the storeroom "out back." If the item was on a high shelf where the infrequently-called-for items were stored, he used a long pole with a flexible metal pincer at the end that made it possible to lift the desired item down.

When all of the wanted items had been retrieved from the shelves, the clerk wrote the price of each item, in a long column, on a brown paper bag, using a soft lead pencil to do so. Before adding the total, he counted the total number of items in the column and checked this total by recounting the individual items, tapping the rubber eraser at the end of his pencil against each as he did so. He then totaled the column, announced the price, and accepted payment.

How different from grocery shopping today! Grocery stores in the 1930s were very small, numerous, and widely dispersed: today they are large, centralized, and relatively few. in the 1930s household members shopped frequently, almost always from a prepared list, purchasing in any single buying excursion no more than could be conveniently carried home. Today the grocery shopper, as often the husband as the wife, shops once or twice a week, pushing a commodious cart along, buying items from a prepared list as well as making unanticipated "impulse" purchases as the whim strikes, as it frequently does. And of course all of this is done without a clerk's help, in row after row of amply stocked shelves and refrigerated cases.

Although the first self-service food store—Piggly Wiggly—appeared in Memphis in the early 1920s, the widespread development of food "supermarkets" did not occur until the wave of suburbanization following World War II.

The basic notion of self-service ultimately spread through a wide range of retail outlets: hardware stores; liquor stores; drugstores; apparel stores; bookstores; candy stores—into any kind of retailing that can be carried on without a clerk interface. It also spread—in many product lines—into mail order catalogues where shopping was accomplished not only without the aid of a clerk, but also without the necessity of a trip to the store.

Today, clerk service is required only in those retail transactions where either some sort of intermediate preparation is required, as in fast-food outlets, or where some sort of expertise is needed, as in opticians', specialized cosmetic, and butcher shops, or pharmacies. In addition, when the value of the individual transaction is very large, as in the case of furs, gems, and automobiles, retail clerks may also play a role: but even in such instances, unaided customer appraisal and selection of merchandise has permeated much of this specialized shopping, too.

Clerk service does linger on in a few grocery and drugstores and other retail outlets, to be sure, but these outlets could just as well be converted to self-service. The holdouts—often in affluent neighborhoods—offer either specialized service (home delivery, credit) or are merely "Mom and Pop" anachronisms that reflect the strength of proprietor personality rather than innate marketing need.

A REVOLUTION IN RETAILING

Self-service liberates package–goods retailing from a very fundamental constraint—the limitation of restricted space. Restricted space limits the amount and kind of merchandise that may be stocked by the individual store. Clerk-service retailing is limited by the average distance the clerk must walk to retrieve the item that the customer wants. The longer the walk, the more inefficient the store.

Self-service retailing is limited only by the distance that a customer is willing to push a cart, or to walk to inspect alternative merchandise choices. In food retailing, where the largest self-service units exist, this limit has apparently yet to be reached. Thus the number of merchandise items that a retail outlet may display to its customers is no longer restricted.

The move to self-service was a dramatic and visible response to a revolution that was taking place in consumer goods retailing. Self-service permitted retail stores to grow in size. Meanwhile, the population and its disposable income were exploding and moving out of the central cities to the suburbs and beyond. Consumer shopping tended, in these suburbs and exurbs, to depend no longer upon a daily or every-other day walk to the nearby retail outlet. Now the shopping trip was typically a weekly drive to a central shopping location which usually featured several and, as shopping malls developed, even scores of retail stores.

Retailers scrambled to keep up with these developments. They moved, following their customers to the suburbs and exurbs. They built fewer, larger self-service stores in order to adapt to the new, automobile-based shopping habits of their clientele. Exhibit 4–1 shows trends in the number of retail food stores in the United States from 1957 to 1988. In this period, the total number of retail food stores *declined* from 327,760 in 1958 to 170,000 in 1988 (as estimated by the A.C. Nielsen Company). Meanwhile, the number of retail-chain food stores increased by 2.5 times from 20,257 in 1957 to 52,000 in 1988. And independent stores decreased by more than half, dropping from 307,403 in 1957 to 118,000 in 1988.

Obviously, the retail food chains thrived in this environment of change. The impact of such chains on total food-store volume was especially dramatic. As Exhibit 4–2 shows, the portion of total food-store sales volume accounted for by the chains increased from 46.5 percent in 1957 to 71.2 percent in 1988.

Similar trends to those seen for food stores developed in most package-goods categories: no increase in the number of stores (usually there were fewer); larger stores; and greater chain influence. In many consumer-durable categories the rise of the discount and mass merchandise stores exacerbated these trends. In automobile retailing there were fewer dealers, larger dealerships, and broader affiliations with automobile manufacturers.

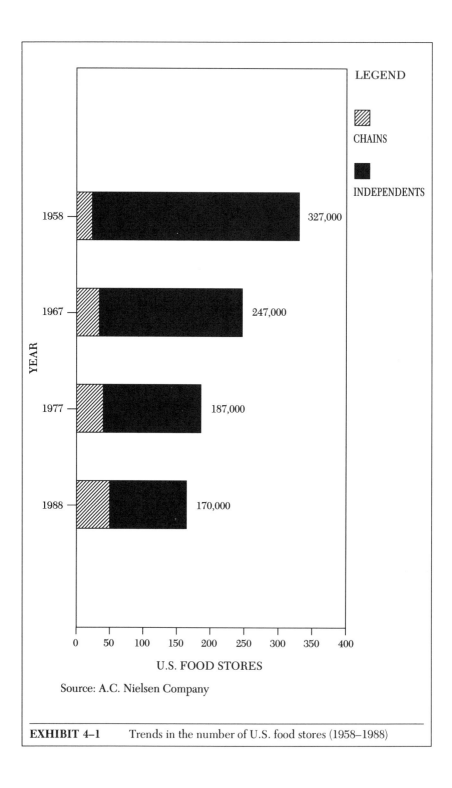

CHAINS

INDEPENDENTS

1958   327,000

1967   247,000

1977   187,000

1988   170,000

YEAR

0   50   100   150   200   250   300   350   400

U.S. FOOD STORES

Source: A.C. Nielsen Company

EXHIBIT 4–1   Trends in the number of U.S. food stores (1958–1988)

CHAIN 46.5%

INDEPENDENT 53.5%

1958

CHAIN 55.9%

INDEPENDENT 44.1%

1967

CHAIN 65.8%

INDEPENDENT 34.2%

1977

CHAIN 71.2%

INDEPENDENT 28.8%

1988

Source: A.C. Nielsen Company

EXHIBIT 4–2   Chain share of total food-store volume (1958–1988)

THE IMPACT OF LARGE/CHAIN STORES IN FOOD RETAILING

As we reflect on these trends in food store retailing, the decisive implication is that of explosive growth in the amount of shelf space per store. As shelf space increases, the retailer may respond in one of four ways:

1. One option for the retailer, and certainly an unlikely one, is to leave the new space unfilled.

2. A second option is to stock the same items that have been stocked historically, but to stock more units of each.For example, the retailer might increase the shelf space allotted to particularly popular items like Campbell's Chicken Noodle Soup or Kellogg's Corn Flakes.

3. A third option is to stock more brands.

4. A final option is to stock a more general assortment of merchandise.

The unanimous decision of food and drug retailers has been to adopt both the third and fourth options. This began to be true in the 1960s and continued explosively in the 1970s and 1980s as ever-larger stores opened with ever-more shelf space.

The statistical picture becomes muddled at just this point. We do not know the precise proportion of non-food store sales in food stores. That the sales of these non-traditional items are substantial is obvious—one has only to walk through the aisles of a contemporary food supermarket and observe the amount of floor space devoted to non-traditional items in these stores.

However, our concern is less with this expansion of non-traditional items in food supermarkets than with the impact of increased retail shelf space on the marketing efforts of food manufacturers and health and beauty aid manufacturers. Specifically, our interest lies with how these marketing activities have affected the brand choices available to consumers in traditional, food retail outlets.

As more shelf space became available, marketers' motives and retailers' motives interacted in an almost perfect harmony: marketers were inclined to provide more brands and brand variants, and because their stores were increasing in size, retailers were able to accept them.

The typical clerk-service store of the 1930s and 1940s stocked a very limited number of brands in any one product category—usually only one in many product categories, but sometimes two or even three in large-volume, marketing-intensive categories. Thus there would likely be one brand of soup or mayonnaise or spaghetti and two or three brands of breakfast cereals or clothes-washing products.

As self-service began to dominate package-goods retail outlets, the number of brands carried increased, apparently in rough proportion to the amount of retail space available. By the early 1960s, for example, when the average food store had about 27 percent more sales in constant dollars than in 1958, marketers expected that most stores would stock no more than three brands in all but the most marketing-intensive categories. These three brands would be the market leader, a second brand–either second in sales and/or a brand that was distinctly different from the market leader–and a "store" brand. The "store" brand was usually a low-priced knock-off of the market leader.

By the late 1980s, the average food store was selling more than three times as much—in constant dollars—as it had in the late 1950s. An explosion in brand stocking, especially in the largest stores, had by now become commonplace.

For example, between 1979 and 1989, *Business Week* reported that "the number of items stocked by a typical supermarket has risen to 26,000 from 13,000."[1]

A substantial portion of this item explosion is accounted for by a proliferation of brands, and by a proliferation of brand variants. Perhaps the best way to appreciate the pervasiveness of brand proliferation is to walk down the aisles of a contemporary supermarket and note the number of different brands and brand variations that are for sale in product category after product category.

The evolution from three-brand stocking in the early 1960s to the brand glut of the late 1980s was not an easy one. Marketers increased pressure on retailers to stock more and more brands as it became more and more obvious that this was a successful way to increase manufacturers' sales and profits, at least temporarily. Retailers acceded to this pressure slowly but surely as they decided collectively to increase the shelf capacity in stores thhhhat they remodeled and in the new stores that they built.

Five factors were the primary causes of this evolution—three affecting particularly the marketers' side and two the retailers':

1. The first factor was the early success of the multi-brand marketers: P&G is the most conspicuous example. P&G marketed 13 advertised brands in 1950. By 1991, this number had increased to over 100. As P&G methodically increased the number of product categories in which it had brand entries as well as the number of its brands and

brand variants in these categories, it became a role model for a whole generation of marketers.

P&G and its followers believed that the way to increase sales and profits was to increase the number of brand entities that were marketed. That P&G was, initially, more successful than most companies in the implementation of this strategy was undoubtedly because the company insisted that each new brand be based on a clearly differentiated and competitively superior product.

2. The second factor that powered the expansion in the number of brands was the powerful influence of technological innovation, brand refinement, brand segmentation, and brand extension. As we have seen, these influences were driven by marketer belief in the force of technology itself, belief in the brand life cycle, belief in the segmentability of consumer markets, and belief in the adaptability of brands to line extensions. In the process, thousands of new brands and brand variants were born.

3. A third factor that caused brand expansion was the discovery by marketers, at least 30 years ago, that it was possible to gently coerce, if not force, the retail trade to stock an increasing number of brands. Brand advertising could cause store customers to request that brand. Similarly, brand coupons (price off or free) or brand samples distributed door-to-door or through the postal system could cause customers to insist that their store stock the couponed or sampled brand.

The initial implication of self-service is a distinct loss in the retailers' ability to influence the brand purchases and preferences of the consumer. Self-service implies that the consumer's choice of brand can depend only upon what that consumer has come to know about the brand prior to exposure to it in the retail store. Thus, as the marketer created brand knowledge and preference through communication with consumers outside the retail environment, the retailer either stocked the item that the customer preferred or risked alienation of the customer base.

4. A fourth factor was the retailer realization that consumers apparently enjoyed shopping in large stores and in stores with a relatively wide selection of merchandise. It was easier and more pleasurable for consumers to shop in stores that offered a large variety of non-food merchandise in addition to food; in stores that emphasized a wide selection of fresh produce and meat; in stores that incorporated

bakeries, pharmacies, video cassette rentals and whatnot; and in stores that offered a wide variety of brands in every food and health and beauty aid category. Retailers were encouraged to expand the size of their stores because of the very favorable customer response to such expanded facilities.

5. Finally, it became evident to the retailer as the number of available brands burgeoned, that retail space, no matter how it expanded, would always be in short supply relative to the number of brands that required it. Retailers always fill the space that is available for a product category. If a new brand is to be accommodated in this space, the retailer must either decrease the amount of space occupied by one or more of the brands that are already there; drop one of those brands; or expand the total space allocated to the product category.

RETAIL SPACE AS A PROFIT CENTER

The increasingly chain-dominated food retail scene was peculiarly able to exploit this situation. It is estimated that food chains are offered over 3,000 new products every year. A typical chain may take on somewhere between 300 and 500 of these items. In this situation it soon became obvious, particularly to chain food retailers, that marketers would be willing to pay in order to ensure that their new brands appear on retail shelves.

Thus, acceptance of new brands became a source of retailer revenue particularly through cash payments for the shelf space itself (slotting allowances), as well as through introductory deals (one free with three); postponed billing or extended credit (dating); or payment for retailer advertising or promotion in support of the new brand; or combinations of these kinds of payoffs.

In addition, retailers realized that their profits could also be enhanced by demanding incentives to maintain shelf presence for brands that had already been permitted shelf access. As a result, increased promotional support was required for older brands, particularly marginal sellers, to maintain them "in stock" on retail shelves. As the number of brands proliferated, not even the established market leaders were immune from this retailer pressure.

Of course, many of these payments to the trade were not new, except for slotting allowances and stocking allowances. But the retail trade did not hold back in the level of its dollar demands for such accommodation. In addition, the level of payments for historic kinds of trade promotional support also increased.

As this pattern of trade accommodation and dealing accelerated, it was not long before the control of consumer price moved into the hands of the supermarket retailers. Once these retailers controlled the price paid by consumers they were in a position to exert powerful pressure on consumer brand choice, especially among undifferentiated brands and brand variants.

Manufacturers had, historically, controlled consumer brand choice through all the traditional means of marketing—particularly through the development of new products, control of distribution channels, and advertising. Now, these traditional powers were undermined by the retailers. In proliferating brands and brand variants, the manufacturers had, perhaps inadvertently, played into the hands of the retailers, rather than strengthening their control over consumers. Chapter 5 provides a further examination of this transition.

---

[1] "Want Shelf Space at the Supermarket? Ante Up," *Business Week*, August 7, 1989, p. 60.

Chapter 5

Sales Promotion and Retail Brand Availability

> Myth #3. Marketers control the prices that ultimate consumers pay for their products.

As one might expect, the growing power of retailers significantly affected the way in which manufacturers allocated marketing funds among various marketing activities. The trend is toward more trade promotional expenditures.

As James Naber summarized the situation in 1986:

> Very simply, of the 65 percent of total marketing expenditures [then] devoted to sales promotion, over half is dedicated to expenditures with the retail trade to maintain in-store distribution, obtain desirable shelf location, and promote special in-store merchandising support.

> The increased concentration of buying power among fewer and fewer retail-account outlets has substantially increased the retailer's ability to demand the financial support of in-store promotional activities from the manufacturer at the expense of direct consumer activities including both advertising and [consumer] sales promotion.[1]

By 1993 the proportion of total marketing expenditures devoted to trade and consumer promotion probably exceeds 70 percent and may have reached 75 percent. The fraction of this that finds its way into retailers' hands may account for three fifths of that total.

These increases in trade promotional expenditures have, over the long haul, been made at the expense of brand advertising to consumers. That is, as brands proliferated, the power of brand advertising to establish consumer preference for individual brands was no longer strong enough to assure brand access to retail shelves; only direct or indirect payments to retailers themselves could assure such access.

The size and variety of such payments to retailers has grown as the pressure to stock more and more brands has grown. In almost every instance, of course, the marketer does get something tangible in return for the promotional payment to the trade—extra sales volume; distribution of a new product; display place and preference; etc. But there is no fixed relation between the size of the payment made to the retailer and what the marketer gets in return. The size of the payment often depends more upon the size of the retailer and its overall importance to the marketer than upon the actual tangible returns of the payment.

Retailers often argue that some, if not most, of this promotion money benefits consumers as it is passed along to them in the form of lower prices. And undoubtedly this is true, at least some of the time. But in the process the retailer assumes important control over consumer brand choice,

From the marketer's point of view, the growing importance of promotional payments to the food retailing trade erodes marketing power in three ways:

1. The retail trade has effectively diverted advertising (and even profit) money from the marketer's use. The marketer has surrendered control over some portion of its marketing funds.

2. The trade no longer perceives that it must stock every brand or brand variant offered by a particular marketer in order to satisfy its customers.

3. The trade decides which brands or brand variants it will offer to its customers. It also decides which brands and brand variants it will offer to its customers at reduced price. To the extent that consumers select brands on the basis of price, the trade has preempted the marketer's power to influence brand selection.

REALITY IN FOOD-STORE RETAILING

No matter how all these forces play themselves out, the consumer now has an extraordinarily wide choice of brands in virtually every product category in retail food stores. What brands are on display and how they are priced is increasingly a decision that is made by the retailer, heavily influenced by the marketer's willingness to make the promotional payments that the trade requires. Whatever the mechanics involved, the end result is that the consumer is deluged with brand and brand variant choices.

The simplest way to understand how these forces have worked to reinforce each other today is to walk down the aisles of a food or drug supermarket and note the myriad brand offerings in category after category. Exhibit 5–1, for example, shows the degree of brand proliferation in the heavy-duty powdered-detergent product category.

Another way to assess the impact of these forces is to trace the distribution history of brands, product category by product category.

One marketing research firm, SAMI, has reported the movement of brands into retail food stores. Since 1979, SAMI has singled out the brands in each product category that achieve at least $1,000,000 in sales each year. Based on everything else that we have seen in this chapter, the obvious expectation is that there has been a significant increase in the number of million-dollar brands between 1979 and 1989. Indeed, this is just what has happened, even after the effect of inflation is eliminated by using constant 1979 dollars.

For example:

- In the canned-soup category, the number of million-dollar brands and brand variants has increased 42 percent, from 12 brands in 1979 to 17 brands in 1989.

- In the brewed ground-coffee category, the number of million-dollar brands and brand variants has increased 58 percent, from 33 brands in 1979 to 52 brands in 1989.

- In the toothpaste category, the number of *food-store* million-dollar brands and brand variants has increased 210 percent, from 10 brands in 1979 to 31 brands in 1989.

- In the ready-to-eat cereal category, there were 84 million-dollar brands and brand variants in 1979 and 150 brands in 1989, an increase of 79 percent.

EXHIBIT 5–1   Heavy-duty powdered-detergent brands—1992

- In the single-strength juice category, there were 17 million-dollar brands and brand variants in 1979 and 39 brands in 1989, an increase of 129 percent.

- In the internal-analgesic category there were 18 million-dollar brands and brand variants in 1979 and 27 brands in 1989, an increase of 89 percent.

To show this brand proliferation in concrete terms, Exhibits 5–2 and 5–3 list million-dollar brands for 1979 and 1989 in two of these categories–toothpaste and brewed ground coffee.

1979:	1989:
Crest	*Crest
Gleem	Crest Tartar Control
Colgate	*Colgate
Ultra brite	Colgate Tartar Control
Close-up	*Aqua-fresh Triple
Pepsodent	Aqua-fresh Tartar Control
Sensodyne	*Close-up
Pearl Drops	Crest for Kids
Aim Gel	*Aim Gel
Aqua-fresh Triple	*Ultra brite
	*Sensodyne
	Aim Extra Strength
	*Pearl Drops
	Aqua-fresh Kids
	*Gleem
	Arm & Hammer Dental Care
	Topol
	Aim Anti-Tartar
	Viadent
	Close-up Tartar Control
	Oral B Muppett
	Colgate Jr
	Close-up Paste
	Check Up
	Pepsodent with Fluoride
	Caffree
	Zact
	Denquil
	Dentagard
	*Pepsodent
	Toms

* As the asterisks indicate, all of the 1979 brands also appear in the 1989 list.

EXHIBIT 5–2   Million-dollar toothpaste brands (constant 1979 dollars)—1979 and 1989

1979:	1989:
Brim	*Folgers
Maxwell House	*Maxwell House
Sanka	Maxwell House Master Blend
Yuban	Folgers Special Roast
Folgers	Folgers Decaffeinated
Chase & Sanborn	*Hills Brothers Red
French Market	*Chock Full of Nuts
Brown Gold	Maxwell House Decaffeinated
Chock Full of Nuts	*Yuban
Butternut	*Sanka
Maryland Club	*Hills Brothers High Yield
S & W	*Chase & Sanborn
JFG	*Brim
Medaglia D'Oro	*MJB Green
Savarin	Hills Brothers Brown Decaffeinated
Stewart's	*Savarin
CDM	*Maryland Club
Melitta	*Butternut
Martinson	Hills Brothers 100% Colombian
Bustelo	*Melitta
Cafe El Pico	*MJB 100% Colombian
High Point	Maxwell House Private Collection
Mr. Automatic	MJB Premium Decaffeinated
American Ace	Brim Dark
Folgers Flaked	*Martinson
Hills Brothers High Yield	*Medaglia d'Oro
Safari	Bonus Blend
MJB 100% Colombian	Chock Full of Nuts Ultra Blend
Butternut Extra	MJB 100% Naturally Decaffeinated
Luzianne Premium Blend	*Cafe El Pico
Luzianne Red Label	*JFG
Hills Brothers Red	MJB Super Yield
MJB Green	Red Diamond
	*Luzianne Red Label
	*Brown Gold
	*Stewart's
	*Safari
	MJB Special Blend

EXHIBIT 5–3   Million-dollar coffee brands in food supermarkets (constant 1979 dollars)—1979 and 1989

(Continued)

> *S&W
> Taster's Choice
> *French Market
> *Mr. Automatic
> MJB European
> *Luzianne Premium Blend
> *CDM
> MJB European Decaffeinated
> Community
> Hills Brothers Gold
> Maryland Club Custom Roast
> Taster's Choice Decaffeinated
> Folgers Gourmet Supreme
> Cafe Pilon
>
> * As the asterisks indicate, 5 of the 1979 million-dollar brands were not on the 1989 list: High Point; Bustelo; American Ace; Folgers Flaked; and Butternut Extra.

There were increases in the physical volume of product sold (pounds, packages, etc.) in some of these categories, to be sure, but the increase in the number of million-dollar brands in the ten-year period *always* exceeded the increase in the physical volume of product sold and usually exceeded it by a very significant amount, as Exhibit 5–4 shows.

And, of course, a single brand or brand variant is frequently available in more than one flavor or variety. Thus, for example, in 1989, SAMI reported that the canned-soup category was composed of a total of 89 brands (million-dollar brands and other) represented by 1,101 separate flavors and/or varieties. Similarly, in the internal-analgesic category in 1989, there were a total of 77 brands and 792 individual varieties for consumers to choose among.

Not all brands, brand variants, or their assorted flavors and varieties are available in most retail outlets, to be sure. But the growth in the number of million-dollar brands, as well as the multiple flavors and varieties in which they are available, reflects the final impact of brand and brand-variant proliferation in the retail food store.

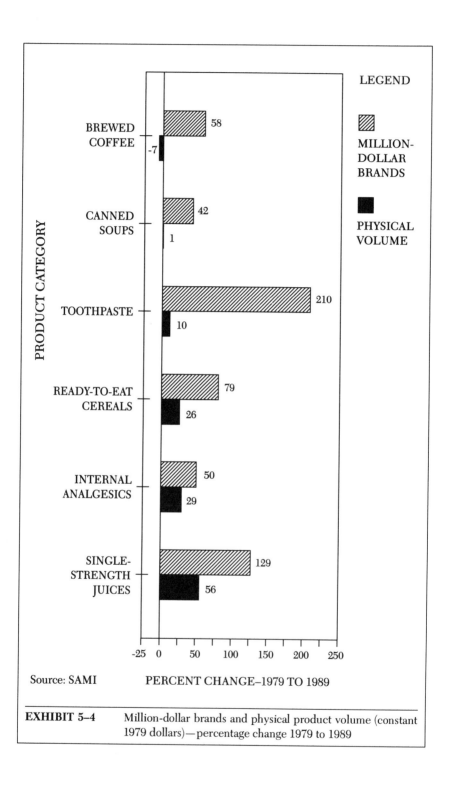

LEGEND

MILLION-DOLLAR BRANDS

PHYSICAL VOLUME

PRODUCT CATEGORY

BREWED COFFEE — 58 / -7

CANNED SOUPS — 42 / 1

TOOTHPASTE — 210 / 10

READY-TO-EAT CEREALS — 79 / 26

INTERNAL ANALGESICS — 50 / 29

SINGLE-STRENGTH JUICES — 129 / 56

-25   0   50   100   150   200   250

Source: SAMI   PERCENT CHANGE–1979 TO 1989

EXHIBIT 5–4   Million-dollar brands and physical product volume (constant 1979 dollars)—percentage change 1979 to 1989

CONSUMER DURABLE RETAILING

It is easy enough to accept all of the foregoing evidence of brand prolifer-ation, shrug one's shoulders, and say, "Well, of course, that's package goods, they're a special case because of self-service. This doesn't have anything to do with all the other non-package-goods categories where self-service is not a factor."

Is this really true?

It is, of course, important to realize that so-called package goods ac-count for at least 28 percent of all retail sales. So package goods are import-ant in their own right. But the facts also suggest that the phenomenon of brand proliferation is not limited to package goods, nor to retail outlets that depend upon self-service.

Take, for example, the automotive category. It accounts for approx-imately 23 percent of all retail sales. Trend statistics at the automobile *dealer* level are essentially parallel to the statistics for food retailers that we have just seen: a decline in the number of dealers in the past thirty years; and each dealer doing a considerably greater volume of business.

- The number of automobile dealerships declined about 19 percent, from a total of 30,800 in 1970 to 25,000 in 1988.[2]

- There has been a steady increase in sales per dealership in constant (1970) dollars. Thus, the average dealership had annual sales of $1,681,818 in 1970, and this had increased about 2.3 times by 1988 to an annual average of $3,945,370 per dealership.[3]

As before, we are struck with the impressive growth in the pro-ductivity of retailing, in this case automotive retailing. But the interesting question, once again, has to do with the nature of this increased volume per dealer. Does it simply represent more sales of essentially the same number of products, or has the number of products available increased?

In fact, the number of available products has increased.

For example, in 1960 the Oldsmobile division of General Motors Cor-poration marketed three different brands of automobiles. In 1992, as Exhibit 5–5 shows, Oldsmobile marketed 17 different lines or brands of autos.

Even though the number of brands and brand variants now changes only slightly from automobile to automobile from year to year, the funda-mental fact is that there has been a vast increase in the number of car brands and brand variants available to the American consumer in the last thirty years. And this increase has occurred in a retail environment that still depends, for better or worse, on salesperson service to the customer.

1960:	1992:
Dynamic 88	Achieva:
Super 88	Sport Coupe
Ninety-Eight	SL
	S
	Bravada
	Custom Cruiser
	Cutlass Ciera:
	SL
	S
	Cutlass Cruiser SL
	Cutlass Supreme:
	International Series
	SL
	S
	Eighty-Eight:
	Royale LS
	Royale
	Ninety-Eight:
	Touring Sedan
	Regency Elite
	Silhouette
	Toronado Torfeo

Source: Oldsmobile History Center.

EXHIBIT 5–5   Oldsmobile automobile car brands—1960 and 1992

Taking all the products of Ford (Ford, Mercury, and Lincoln), the increase has been from 15 brands in 1960 to 50 in 1992. The comparable figures for all of General Motors (Chevrolet, Pontiac, Oldsmobile, Buick, and Cadillac) are 21 in 1960 and over 65 in 1992. To fully appreciate the proliferation of branded automobile entities available, one would have to add in all the Chrysler products, and all of the products of Japanese, German, and other automobile manufacturers who export their products into the American automobile market. One estimate puts the total number of automobile brands and brand variants available to the American consumer at around 700 in 1992.

The simple segmentation approach of General Motors' Alfred P. Sloan —"a car for every purse and purpose"—has become a mockery of itself. As one automobile dealer expressed the current situation from his perspective:

"You've got a half-a-dozen different car models and just as many trucks and vans," he said, "and all of them have different packages of features, options, and price points. It's really just too much for most people to carry all of this around in their heads, especially when they're demonstrating one product one minute and a completely different one 10 or 15 minutes later."[4]

The automotive-product category suffers from a severe case of over-segmentation and excessive line extension. Segments/extensions have been devised on the most tenuous grounds. In addition, the manufacturers themselves have imagined, arrogantly, that markets exist for cars that they can easily make, rather than for cars that consumers will buy.

If anything, there has been at least as much brand proliferation in the salesperson-dependent automobile field in the past 30 years as in the self-service-dependent package-goods fields. Perhaps this is because the franchised automobile dealers have to more or less accept the products that manufacturers deliver to them. In automobiles there is less friction in the distribution system—less backward pressure than we have witnessed in the food trade.

But less backward pressure in the system has not prevented a form of trade promotion from developing in the automobile industry. Dealer-incentive programs and manufacturer-sponsored zero- or low-interest rate automobile loans both put pressure on automobile list prices and divert consumer attention from brand distinctiveness to price differentiation. These programs may be linked to particular car brands or brand variants, or they may be generally available across a manufacturer's line. But no matter how they are used, such trade promotion programs have become necessary because there is, on average, so little perceivable difference among automobile brands with comparable list prices.

Taken together, automobile and package goods account for at least half of all retail sales in the United States. But the proliferation of brands and brand variations has not been limted to these two product categories. Many, if not most, other product categories have shown similar explosions during the past three decades in the number of brands and brand variations that they offer to the consumer.

Consider, for example, brand proliferation in the alcoholic beverage, consumer electronic equipment, apparel, and consumer appliance categories.

In each of these categories, marketers demonstrate their fundamental conviction that the way to increase sales and profits is to increase the number of brands and brand variants that they make available to consumers.

And in each of these categories the retailer has accommodated the marketer by accepting an ever-increasing number of brands.

But not all new brands can be succcessful, and more important, only a very few if any can achieve decisive market dominance.

It is a truism that the more brands and brand variants there are in a market, the less the average difference between individual brands can be. As differences disappear or become minimal or inconsequential, brands seem to be more and more the same. Brands that are so much alike as to seem the same are called commodities.

Of course marketers did not set out to achieve a marketplace composed of myriad similar brands. Each of them set out, one would presume, to create a marketplace composed of dominant brands.

Unhappily, most individual manufacturers have not been able to impose enough discipline upon their marketing efforts to produce dominant brands. The final effect of all their marketing effort and marketing expenditure has been to produce myriad brands and brand variants, no one of which is or can come to be dominant in its market.

As Bill Boswell and Dick Zenko put it:

> There's not very much difference between products today. We like to think that there are [sic] in reaction to a lot of marketing hype, but the fact remains that most products out there are fairly similar.[5]

Contemporary marketers have been well accommodated by the retail trade. All the many brand and brand variant refinements, segmenters, and extenders can find their way into the expanded retail facilities in consumer goods categories; in consumer durable categories; and many other merchandise categories. At least they can find their way if the marketer is willing to pay the price that the retailer demands for their presence.

Many marketers believe that advertising will resolve the problems of proliferated brands. Discipline in marketing means, to these marketers, heightened advertising creativity—advertising creativity that will differentiate brands that are, in reality, commodities. Such advertising will be, these marketers believe, so powerful that consumers will want to buy the brands that it supports, in spite of their sameness and lack of competitive distinction.

It is to the question of the role of advertising in contemporary marketing that we turn in Chapter 6.

---

[1] Naber, James H., "The Sales Promotion Explosion," *James Webb Young Fund Address Series*, Department of Advertising, University of Illinois, Urbana–Champaign, 1986, p. 15.

[2] *Statistical Abstract of the United States*, U.S. Department of Commerce, Bureau of the Census, Washington, D.C., 1990, Table 1373.

[3] Ibid. (Table 1373 provided sales data. Constant dollar calculations supplied.)

[4] Doody, Alton F., and Ron Bingaman, *Reinventing the Wheels*, Harper & Row, New York, 1988, pp. 99-100.

[5] Boswell, Bill, and Dick Zenko, "Advertising Versus Promotion–How to Maximize the Balance," *Advertising Management Conference Showcase*, Association of National Advertisers, Inc., New York, 1990, p. 14.

Chapter 6

The Changing Role of Advertising

> Myth #4. Advertising can solve all marketing problems.

Advertising enjoys a rather special place in the minds of business-people. Many of them seem to believe that if everything else in marketing fails to increase sales and profits, advertising may still be able to do the job. The belief, or hope, is that if advertising will only do its job, contemporary marketing need not worry about other problems. Thus, advertising enjoys its own mystique among businesspeople. They believe that it works to increase sales and profits almost independently of other marketing activities.

Advertising is a corporate activity that is managed on a day-to-day basis to influence the thoughts and actions of consumers. Product innovations, or changes in distribution or even fundamental changes in pricing strategy are relatively infrequent events in the marketing of consumer products. A fundamental change in a branded product or service is an un-usual event. But, at least so marketers believe, it is possible to change the brand's image and the benefits that consumers perceive it to promise through advertising. Advertising can be changed rapidly and continuously: such changes do not necessarily depend upon other changes in the brand or its marketing circumstances.

No matter what businesspeople believe, the actual effects of advertising on sales and profits are usually unpredictable. The core attitude of marketers seems to be that although it is almost always impossible to predict the success of a new advertising campaign in advance, there is always the possibility that its effects will be substantial. It might be said that the fundamental appeal of advertising is that it offers the marketer the possibility—no matter how remote it may be—of generating a lot of sales and profits for relatively little money.

Gerard Lambert suggests that hope always springs eternal in the mind of the advertiser:

> I am perfectly aware that some items must have distribution, display, and competitive discounts *above all else*. But there are many products where a dollar can best be spent on advertising and not on free goods, discounts, and deals.[1]

The real question that faces the marketer is whether, when, and to what extent Mr. Lambert's optimism about advertising, at least for "many products," is confirmed in the marketplace.

ADVERTISING ADDS VALUE

What is it that advertising accomplishes—when it works at all? The simple answer is that it enhances the value of the brand that it presents to the public. This addition to the brand's value can, it is argued, come about in four interrelated ways:

1. There is the fact of advertising itself. Advertising can make the consumer aware of the brand. The least that advertising can do is to bring the brand to the attention of the consumer. But there is more to it than simply making the consumer aware—the very fact that the brand is advertised at all is explicit testimony to the manufacturer's belief in the value of the advertised brand. In a very real sense the existence of the advertising constitutes an implied manufacturer's warranty of the value of the brand.

2. Advertising makes the brand seem different from its competitors. The *ways* in which advertising can make a brand seem different from its competitors will receive a lot more attention in what follows. For the moment, however, we are simply concerned with the fact that the advertising message—whatever it may be—is designed to make a brand seem different from its competitors. If the difference that is portrayed by the advertising makes the brand seem better, then it will be

perceived by consumers to be more valuable than the brands against which it competes.

Of course, it is at just this point that reality intervenes in the development of brand value added through advertising. The advertising is ultimately limited by the actual performance characteristics of the brand. Advertising cannot imply a value that the brand cannot deliver for to do so will, sooner or later, defeat the purpose of the advertising itself.

So in the final analysis the value that advertising can add to the brand is limited by the characteristics of the brand and by the imagination of the advertising's creator. The creator must find ways to make the brand *seem* different that are not inconsistent with the brand's inherent characteristics.

3. The idea of value added by advertising has another important dimension. Value added by advertising works directly upon the consumer—the value is created in the private interaction between advertisement and recipient. To the extent that the consumer makes purchases in a self-service environment, advertising has an unparalleled opportunity for influence.

If the advertising has created a perception of value about the brand in the consumer's mind, there is no other communication about the brand (except price) in the self-service environment of food and drug supermarkets, and self-service liquor, consumer electronic, hardware, stationery, ready-to-wear, sundry, and other such retail outlets to reduce or distort the power of the ideas and associations that advertising has created.

As Alice Goldfarb Marquis put it:

Advertising ... had short-circuited the age-old relationship between buyer and seller. Like every aspect of urban life, shopping became impersonal, solitary, an internal monologue of fantasy and desire on the part of the buyer, triggered by recognition of the advertised brand name.[2]

Even in non-self-service product categories such as automotive, consumer durable, jewelry, and other salesperson-intensive retail environments, the value added by advertising can determine the brands that the consumer comes to consider and, thus, the specific retail establishments that the consumer decides to visit. It can also determine specific brands or brand variants that the consumer will attend to within that retail establishment.

4. Finally, if the advertising for a product does add value to it, the product may be sold for a higher and more stable price than if a consumer perceives it to be no different from the products with which it competes.

In the best of all advertising worlds:

> Low price alone is not enough to dislodge a brand leader fortified by perceived added value. Sometimes this truth is overlooked by marketers caught in the squeeze between manufacturing costs and retail price points.[3]

When advertising is effective in making a product seem different and better, it has in reality accomplished two things for the advertiser:

- It makes the consumer think as the advertiser wishes the consumer to think.

- It predisposes the consumer to act as the advertiser wishes the consumer to act.

THE DIFFERENCE THAT ADVERTISING CAN MAKE

It is obvious that consumer perceptions of differences between brands caused by advertising are the essence of the advertising opportunity. The more that advertising can make a brand seem different and better, the more effect advertising can have on the sales of that brand.

Where do these differences that advertising attempts to create come from? They come from two sources: from the product itself and from the characteristics that advertising creates for the product.

Differences Between Brands

If a brand is distinctly different from its competitors—think of the first Sony compact disc changer with the discs resting on a lazy-susan-like tray or of the Gillette "sensor" razor—advertising will describe such inherent brand differences.

A good deal of contemporary consumer advertising reflects brand differences that are so slight that one may wonder whether consumers will consider them to add distinctive value to the brand. In fact, many advertising practitioners believe that the secret of effective advertising is to identify, for every product or service, what Rosser Reeves called its "unique selling proposition" or "USP."[4]

In a sense, this question of meaningless differences is not an advertising question at all, but rather a question of brand development strategy. The important point, of course, is that many marketers accept intrinsic brand differences as the *only* acceptable basis for advertising, no matter now insignificant the difference may be.

No matter what the reason for the proliferation of brands with relatively insignificant or meaningless competitive differences, the plain fact of the matter is that when advertising is based solely on *intrinsic* brand differences, the potential success of the advertising depends solely on consumer perceptions of the importance—value to them—of the brand difference that the advertising portrays.

Differences Between Advertisements

The alternative source of brand differentiation comes from advertising itself. These *extrinsic* brand differences, created by advertising, have produced some of the greatest advertising success stories of all time.

Marlboro is not an *intrinsically* different cigarette product than its competitors, no matter what virtues its manufacturer may ascribe to its tobacco, or paper, or filter. But Marlboro advertising deals with none of these product-based virtues. It deals instead with an advertising created abstraction about the brand—Marlboro Country. What Marlboro means to consumers today is what the executions over a 30-odd-year period of this distinctive, brilliant advertising concept have taught consumers about Marlboro.

Similarly, the "Pepsi Generation" has nothing to do with the characteristics of the Pepsi–Cola product. It may very well be that Pepsi–Cola is different from and, in the view of some consumers, better than Coca–Cola. But Pepsi Generation advertising and the singular success that it has given Pepsi–Cola has nothing to do with its superiority, as a product, to Coca–Cola. The Pepsi Generation advertising is concerned only with the people who drink the product. According to the advertising, Pepsi–Cola is the soft drink of choice for younger, less inhibited, up-beat, contemporary members of the population—the very people, it might be added, who are the most likely consumers of carbonated cola beverages in the first place.

Of course, the great bulk of advertising combines the intrinsic characteristics of the brand advertised with the extrinsic characteristics of the brand. These are added by advertising in order to make the advertised brand seem distinctive and, thus, more valuable.

The original advertising for Lite beer is a case in point. Lite is a differentiated beer product: it contains fewer calories than conventional beers. The difference in calories—96 calories in a twelve-ounce can of Lite versus about 150 calories for conventional beers—provides an advertisable difference.

The original Lite advertising, created by the Backer & Spielvogel advertising agency, brilliantly exploited this product difference—"More taste, less filling. Everything you've always wanted in a beer and less."—in the context of ebullient, aging, and, frequently, overweight retired athletes.

The power of the extrinsic advertising idea can be isolated in this example by contrasting it with advertising created for a virtually identical product—Gablinger Beer—that was marketed some years before Lite. Gablinger was presented simply as a low-calorie beer in a straightforward, more or less factual exposition of the intrinsic product characteristics.

Lite, of course, proved an outstanding marketing success, and Gablinger proved a rather dismal failure.

It is probably true that there are as many creative solutions to advertising problems as there are creative advertising people. The key issue in every advertising problem is, nevertheless, how to add value to the product through advertising, and the fundamental choice to be made in adding such value is whether to do it through an emphasis upon intrinsic product characteristics or through the creation of extrinsic advertising assertions about the brand, and in what combination and with what emphasis.

Once made, this fundamental decision influences every other advertising decision that will ever be made for the brand. That is, the original advertising decision for a brand restrains the advertiser in all subsequent decisions about advertising the intrinsic and extrinsic characteristics of the brand. Consumer perceptions are not infinitely malleable. Once the advertiser starts down one advertising path with a brand—let us say by emphasizing a particular product characteristic—a limit is placed on the kinds of things that can be asserted about the brand in future advertising.

And so the perceptions that consumers hold in their minds about a brand tend to constrain new advertising initiatives. When a brand is totally new, consumers have a clean slate in their minds about it. The first advertising in behalf of the brand fills this slate, hopefully—if the advertising is well conceived—with a clear and simple reflection of what the brand is, and a clear and compelling promise of what its value to the consumer will be.

Subsequent advertising must be both credible in terms of the advertising that has gone before but must also extend and reinforce the existing consumer perception of the brand. Thus, every time a *new* advertising solution is sought for a brand, that solution must deal not only with the intrinsic characteristics of the brand and the extrinsic characteristics of *past* advertising about the brand but also with what the consumer has made of them. It is very difficult—some advertising people would say virtually impossible—to restructure fundamentally, through subsequent advertising, what the consumer has learned about the value of a product through old advertising.

If subsequent advertising about the brand is particularly effective, it almost certainly has not changed the basic assertion that has been made by the old advertising.

Advertising campaigns that vacillate back and forth between intrinsic and extrinsic product characteristics, or that switch back and forth from one intrinsic or extrinsic approach to another, almost inevitably redefine the value that advertising adds to the product. This will blur and, ultimately, extinguish whatever difference, if any, advertising has created for the brand in the first place.

This combination of factors defines the problem that all advertising practitioners face as they set out to create new advertising for an old brand. The process, and its inherent difficulties, are well illustrated by the advertising history of Alka-Seltzer, the effervescent antacid/analgesic product that was introduced in the 1930s. Alka-Seltzer's intrinsic product characteristics remained essentially the same until a reformulated version was introduced in 1989.

In the early years, the advertising for Alka-Seltzer was based on a cartoon character called "Speedy" who extolled the fast relief that Alka-Seltzer offered for symptoms of stomach distress and overindulgence. A typical "Speedy" commercial is shown in Exhibit 6–1.

Speedy retired in the early 1960s and was replaced by a series of commercials that humorously presented Alka-Seltzer as the means of relief for a wide range of symptoms—one symptom per commercial. The symptoms included not only stomach upset and overindulgence, but also headaches, colds, and a generalized low-level feeling of discomfort called the "blahs." A commercial about the "blahs" and Alka-Seltzer is shown in Exhibit 6–2.

In this series Alka-Seltzer was presented as the remedy of choice by professional pie eaters—men who "overeat for a living." It offered relief to characters who felt vaguely ill at ease but could not identify exactly what was wrong with them; and was preferred by cartoon stomachs whose masters

EXHIBIT 6–1

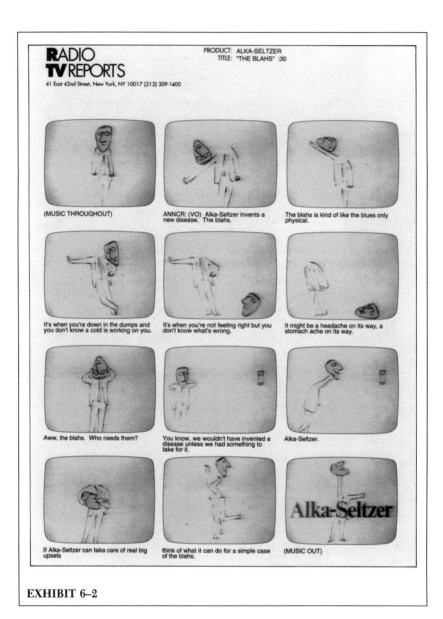

EXHIBIT 6–2

had abused them by eating upsetting foods. All of this added up to a wide range of good-natured fun. The basic premise of the new campaign extended and reinforced the fundamental meaning of the Alka-Seltzer product that had previously been developed and nurtured by "Speedy."

The promise of a broad range of symptomatic relief was somewhat narrowed in the mid- 1960s when a flanker Alka-Seltzer product specifically formulated for the relief of cold symptoms was introduced under the name of Alka-Seltzer Plus. But the advertising for original Alka-Seltzer continued to emphasize relief of all the non-cold symptoms, one to a commercial.

Rulings in 1970 and 1971 by the U.S. Food and Drug Administration established guidelines for antacid advertising dealing with concurrent symptoms. Alka-Seltzer advertising changed course again. The humorous tone remained, but the emphasis was now solely on overindulgence that causes stomach upset—gone were headache relief, the suggestion of over-indulgence in alcoholic beverages, and the "blahs."

In a commercial that epitomized the advertising for the brand in the 1970s, a television actor was shown struggling to achieve a perfect "take" while eating plate after plate of spicy meatballs. As the takes unfold, the ac-tor begins to show the effects of eating too much, and the announcer takes over and extols the virtues of Alka-Seltzer for just such symptoms. In another memorable commercial from this period, "Ralph" sat on the edge of his bed and groaned, "I can't believe I ate the whole thing." (See Exhibit 6–3.)

Thus, in the post "Speedy" period, Alka-Seltzer advertising moved back and forth among the symptoms for which Alka-Seltzer provided relief, expanding at first to a broad range of symptoms and then, responding to the FDA rulings, pulling back to stomach upset.

In the early 1980s both the intrinsic and extrinsic character of Alka-Seltzer advertising changed and changed dramatically. The intrinsic merit of the product was now characterized by a totally new symptom—the stress that accompanies modern living. Totally excluded was the full range of symptoms for which Alka-Seltzer had provided relief in the previous twenty years.

Apparently this change in the definition of the intrinsic value of Alka-Seltzer was based on the belief that overindulgence and stomach dis-tress, as such, were outmoded. Extrinsically, the commercials abandoned overt humor and emphasized instead the jangling disjointedness of contem-porary life that, it was implied, produces the stress that Alka-Seltzer was now said to relieve.

EXHIBIT 6–3

In 1985 there was another change. Alka-Seltzer was now represented as the product that could provide fast relief for overindulgence and, specifically, for acid indigestion—a refinement from the previous emphasis on generalized stomach distress and, quite possibly, from the consumer view yet another new symptom that Alka-Seltzer could address.

As Miles Laboratories president, Edward Guftason, put it in an interview with the *Wall Street Journal*:

Overindulgence and speed of relief are what the brand was built on.[5]

Not only had the brand's intrinsic benefit shifted to acid indigestion, the extrinsic character of the television commercials shifted to hyperbole.

In one of the new commercials a man eats a chili dinner, then sits comfortably reading his newspaper until fire engine bells and sirens sound; his stomach distends and lights up; the newspaper is ignited; and he is obviously in considerable discomfort. The man quickly ingests Alka-Seltzer and then settles back contentedly, a smile on his face, to contemplate the newspaper which now has a large hole burned in it. (See Exhibit 6–4.)

Finally, in 1989, Alka-Seltzer was reformulated with improved flavor, lower sodium content, and aspirin substitute. The advertising changed yet again, reverting to a humorous treatment of overindulgence-caused stomach upset. (See Exhibit 6–5.) As reported by Kim Foltz in the *New York Times*:

One commercial uses the kind of homemade meal gone wrong scenario that Alka-Seltzer made famous. A man and woman are shown groaning at the dinner table as the host asks from the kitchen, "How do you like the meatloaf?" Shocked, one of them says *soto voce*, "That was meatloaf?" Meanwhile the man offers Alka-Seltzer to cure their heartburn.[6]

The point of this little history of Alka-Seltzer advertising is to suggest the dilemma of the advertising creator who is asked to develop a new advertising campaign for a brand with a rich advertising history. The advertising must be fresh and new, of course, but it must also illuminate the difference that the brand possesses and the value that it delivers to the consumer. The basic issue is, always, how can the advertising be fresh and "creative" and yet maintain the original essence of the brand as the consumer has come to perceive it, within an evolving competitive and regulatory environment.

RADIO
TVREPORTS

41 East 42nd Street, New York, NY 10017 (212) 309-1400

PRODUCT: ALKA-SELTZER
TITLE: "BURNING NEWSPAPER" :30

(SFX:SIRENS)

ANNCR:(VO) That chili you had for dinner

has just started a three alarm fire inside you. Alka-Seltzer to the rescue.

Alka-Seltzer goes to work instantly

to take the burn out of your heartburn

(MUSIC)

and also quiet the sirens in your head.

So when your body is sending you smoke signals, send Alka-Seltzer to the rescue and put out the fire fast.

SINGER: ALKA-SELTZER TO THE RESCUE.

EXHIBIT 6–4

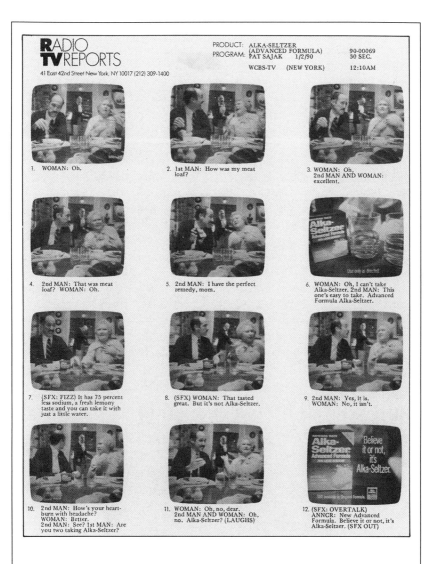

EXHIBIT 6–5

As the machinations of the Alka-Seltzer creative work unfold over the years and the decades, it is clear that consumer perceptions of difference and value—the essence of what the brand has been in the past—are not always maintained and reinforced. Part of this is due to the inherent difficulty of the problem itself, part is due to regulatory issues inherent in the creation of advertising for over-the-counter medicines, and part is undoubtedly due to the passing parade of brand managers and advertising agency creative people who, from time to time, have been assigned the responsibility for the advertising destiny of the brand.

As the advertising history of Alka-Seltzer reveals, it is easy for well meaning and, presumably, intelligent people to fuzz up the essence of the brand; to vacillate from one intrinsic product characteristic to another; and to change the extrinsic nature of Alka-Seltzer from one new advertising campaign to the next. The problem is especially difficult for a brand like Alka-Seltzer because a good deal of its advertising thrust is, presumably, directed at current users. The objective is to maintain their allegiance to the brand over time.

Maintaining fresh and distinctive advertising *continuity* is the fundamental challenge of creative advertising. The Alka-Seltzer advertising history reveals that this is a very difficult task.

It is within this challenge that the ever-bright promise of advertising, as portrayed by its enthusiasts and outlined at the beginning of this chapter, is frequently betrayed.

THE LONG-TERM DECLINE IN ADVERTISING CREATIVITY

If the creators of advertising do not have enough to worry about, their plight is aggravated by the plain fact that they simply do not seem to be as good as they used to be—in the golden days of advertising creativity.

There are at least seven reasons for this long-term decline in advertising creativity.

1. The Advertising Agency Environment

The nature of the environment that exists within advertising agencies for the development of new advertising ideas has changed dramatically. An environment that was once loose, unrestricted, and permissive has become formal, hierarchical, and severe.

Advertising agencies once calculatedly provided an ambience that literally bred great creative insights from an uninhibited band of kindred spirits. As agencies have evolved over the years, a good deal of thought and effort has been devoted to maintaining this ambience, at least within the creative department and, in the larger agencies, within individual creative groups.

But this has not been an easy goal to achieve. The advertising agency business, once a cottage industry that could pursue its destiny pretty much as it wished, has become a *serious business*.

As this transition has occurred, the attitude of those who run advertising agencies has gradually changed. An organization that once thrived on genuine intellectual fun must now act like a successful business; think like a successful business; speak like a successful business; and generate predictable profits like a successful business. This malaise may be especially acute in the publicly-owned agencies, but there is no shortage of seriousness and purposefulness in all agencies these days, no matter how big they are, and no matter how they happen to be owned.

It is different being a creative person in an advertising agency in 1992 than it was in 1950 or 1960 or even 1970. There is, for the creative person, more inhibition, less unrestrained adventure, more structure, and more interaction with other agency and client employees.

Creative work is now done in an environment that is characterized by two organizational flaws:

- There is more irrelevant pressure on the creative people.

- Creative people have less ultimate responsibility for the work that they produce.

As a result of these two factors, the inherent challenge of creativity for creative people has diminished. Also diminished is the ultimate pyschic reward for the creative person's successful advertising insight.

2. The People

This change in environment from loose to structured, unrestrained to severe, has also changed the kind of people who are attracted to the creative side of the advertising agency business. One of the eternal mysteries of advertising agencies is just where creative people come from and just how they find their way into agency creative departments.

Creative jobs—particularly beginning creative jobs—are hard to come by. A major reason for this is that the would-be creators have never proved in past educational pursuits or work experience that they can create effective advertisements. There is no middle ground here and no time for lengthy apprenticeships that may or may not produce a successful end product. One can either create advertisements or not, and it is devilishly hard for the novices to prove, before the event, that they will be able to do the job. The upshot of all this is that most creative people are hired on the basis of the instinct of people who are already employed as creative people.

If the nature of the environment for creative work in advertising agencies has changed, and it has, then the kinds of people who are successful in creative departments have also changed. Those who can best adapt to the evolving environment are most likely to succeed. And when this changing talent pool seeks out young people to help in the creative process, their instinct will be to hire novices that appear to have at least some of the adaptive characteristics that the senior creative person has depended upon for survival and success. As this process unfolds, the kind of creative talent that is available within an advertising agency tends to change—it becomes more adaptive, more political, more compromising. It becomes, in fact, less creative.

3. The Creative Process

The nature of the creative process has become more participative as the years have passed. The great copywriters of the past tended to be loners— people who reached their own solutions to creative problems on their own terms and in their own ways. Such single-mindedness is increasingly difficult to realize in advertising agencies, as more and more people participate in the creative process. And particularly as more and more people—both inside the agency and at the client—are permitted to judge finished creative work.

As hierarchies develop within agencies (creative director, associate creative director, creative group head, senior copywriter, senior art director, copywriter, art director in the creative department; and group management supervisor, management supervisor; senior account manager, account executive, assistant account executive in the account management ranks) and within client organizations as well (vice president—marketing, group product director, product manager, assistant product manager), more and more people participate in one way or another in the development and appraisal of advertising-agency creative work.

At worst, this multiplication of roles in the creative process produces finished work that is bland, broadly acceptable, and lacking in courage and risk. Yet great advertising campaigns are almost always insightful, assertive, often objectionable to a few, and almost always contain some element of risk. Multiplying the number of people who have a say in the creative process has inevitably debased whatever creativity was there to begin with.

4. Copy Testing

Not only must advertising pass muster among an increasing number of its creator's peers and masters, but it is now almost routinely submitted to some sort of quantitative "copy testing." Such copy testing is not without its faults, as we shall see in Chapter 10.

From the standpoint of the creator of advertising, such copy testing imposes another external restraint on the creative work. No matter how rational the copy testing method may appear to be, its results are totally unpredictable and inherently insensitive to the intellectual and emotional basis of the creative work to which they are applied.

5. Personal Contact

As the environment of the advertising agency has evolved, it is no longer the creative person's responsibility to seek insights into consumers' thoughts and perceptions through personal contact.

The great copywriters of the past have been unanimous in stressing such personal contact as the basis for their most impressive creative insights. For example, Leo Burnett said:

> My technique, if I have one, is to saturate myself with knowledge of the product. I believe in good depth interviewing where I come realistically face to face with the people I am trying to sell. I try to get a picture in my mind of the kind of people they are—how they use the product, and what it is—they don't often tell you in so many words—but what it is that actually motivates them to buy something or to interest them in something.[7]

Now this vital developmental process is not done *by* the creative person—it is done *for* the creative person. Information comes to the creative person from all directions—agency researchers, client researchers, agency planners, account executives, brand managers, outside consultants, and research gurus—ad nauseam. In a very real sense, creative people simply do not get their hands dirty with the consumer anymore.

6. Exhaustion of Creative Ideas

Another problem is that constant creative activity on a brand tends, over a period of time, to exhaust the best ideas. The longer a brand is advertised, the fewer first-rate ideas remain to be exploited. So when a change in advertising seems necessary, only mediocre and second-rate ideas remain to be exploited. There are, after all, only so many things that can be said about any brand of anything.

Put yourself, for example, in the position of someone who must write advertising copy for a brand like Alka-Seltzer in 1993. If you start with the problem from scratch, you will almost inevitably come up with ideas that the old hands on the brand—your supervisor or the client brand manager—know have been used before. Alternatively, if you start the creative process by looking at a reel of historic Alka-Seltzer commercials, it is likely that you will be so humbled that your own Alka-Seltzer creative juices will be unable to flow at all.

7. The Consumer

Finally, the consumer has changed. Advertising has become the consumer's constant and intrusive companion. If creative people have trouble finding anything new to say about a brand, the consumer has probably heard it all before anyway—if not from one brand in a product category, then from its competitors.

Not only are consumers world-weary, they are also wise to wiles of the creator of advertising. Advertisements that were especially effective 30 years ago would, in many instances, simply be ignored or laughed at by today's veteran recipient of advertising ideas and advertising ploys.

For all these reasons, the creative product of advertising agencies has deteriorated and will continue to deteriorate. Mostly this is because advertising agencies and their creative product have come of age—the brashness, the uninhibitedness, the dramatic insight that once characterized agency creative work have, to an important degree, disappeared. They have been replaced by a maturity and sense of fiscal responsibility that many advertisers undoubtedly think was too long in coming. In the process, the probability of a creative breakthrough for a given brand, with all else held constant, is simply much lower than it was 30 years ago.

But no matter what has been happening to the creative process and regardless of the increased cynicism of consumers, an important cause of the long-term decline of advertising creativity has been the proliferation of brands and brand variants. As brands and brand variants proliferate, the average difference among them must diminish. There has been a long-term decline in advertising creativity because there has been a long-term decline in brand advertisability. As corporations proliferate brands and brand variants, they create a sameness among brands that emasculates the very advertising that they depend upon to create consumer desire.

CONSUMER PROMOTION DILUTES ADVERTISING EFFECT

Marketers spend a significant and increasing proportion of their marketing funds in promotions directed at influencing consumers directly at the point of sale. They give some sort of added incentive—usually price—to buy a particular brand. These promotional incentives to buy include, especially, price-off coupons as well as price-off packages; refund offers; promotional packages with extra product at "regular" price; in-pack or strap-on premium merchandise; consumer contests; consumer sweepstakes; and so forth.

If the consumer makes a brand choice because of the incentive offered, the incentive has effectively destroyed all that the consumer has learned about the brand and its distinctive qualities through advertising. In addition, such promotional incentives suggest to the consumer that whatever value resides in a particular brand, it is not of sufficient consequence to offset a small incentive offered by the promotion.

Such consumer promotions work best when there are multiple undifferentiated brands in a category. The promotions force consumers to recognize that all the brands in the category are pretty much the same. As Dan Ailloni–Charas put it:

> The more commoditized the product category, the higher the use of coupons is for products in that category.[8]

Marketers use consumer promotions to make sure that the incentives offered accrue directly to their own brands. The more impervious a brand is to price competition, the less likely is a marketer to promote it directly to the consumer. If, however, a brand is sensitive to price competition, the marketer has little choice but to resort to consumer promotion to meet such price competition head on.

When a product is distinctive and valuable to the consumer, it does not require promotional incentives to drive its sales. A case in point is the Ford Explorer utility vehicle. As the *New York Times* reported in 1991:

> One notable success has been the Explorer four-door utility vehicle, which drew rave reviews from automotive enthusiast magazines. The

Explorer has been selling strongly, without any financial incentives or discount programs, since its introduction last year.[9]

When a marketer promotes directly to the consumer, it is a tacit admission that advertising is no longer powerful enough to make the brand seem valuable enough to the consumer to make it invulnerable to modest price reductions.

Just as promotional payments to the trade have diluted the marketer's ability to influence brand choice, so incentive promotions directed at consumers reflect the dilution of advertising's power to influence the brand choice of consumers. Thus, the success of promotions reflects a growing inability of advertising to create the illusion of decisive brand value.

As the marketer creates more and more brands with fewer and fewer competitive differences, the need to provide consumer incentives to create sales accelerates, and the opportunity for advertising to make a meaningful contribution to the brand's success declines.

ADVERTISING'S ROLE IN CONTEMPORARY MARKETING

In the late 1800s, marketing in America was basically concerned with the sales and physical distribution of unbranded products in barrels, crates, and boxes.

As Richard S. Tedlow describes this depressing past:

> There were few proprietary product differences which made the establishment of a brand identity problematic. The consumer lived in a world not of brands but of commodities. Indeed, the consumer market in 1880 was characterized not by packaging but by packing.[10]

The revolution in marketing that branding and advertising has created now seems to have come full circle. If in 1892 there was a tyranny of the packer, there is in 1992 a tyranny of the multiple brand and all that this implies.

In a very real sense the historic dominance of individual brands could not have come about in the absence of advertising. Whatever problems advertising has today—and, as we have seen, they are substantial—the overwhelming problem of advertising is the proliferation of distinctionless brands. Indeed, it is increasingly true in 1992, as it was in 1892, that there are "few proprietary product differences," which makes, once again, "the establishment of a brand identity problematic."

It is certain that breathing advertising life into traditional brands would have become increasingly difficult even if the creators of advertising themselves had not fallen into a funk. But beyond this, the overwhelming reality is that it is very difficult to create the illusion of value for a brand that is essentially identical to its competitors.

In addition, it is virtually certain that the unrestrained promise of advertising—getting substantial marketing success for considerably less than it should cost—has contributed to the problems of contemporary marketing. No one knows just how many marketers blithely proliferate brands on the rosy assumption that advertising can be counted on to make those ever-more-alike brands distinctive and valuable to consumers. In the simplistic days of the 1960s this may very well have been so. But not anymore.

And at the same time, it must be admitted that it is not easy to find anyone in the advertising business that has ever uttered a word of warning about what the proliferation of brands will do to the effectiveness of advertising.

It is certainly more difficult to create truly effective advertising today than ever before, and there certainly is a long-term decline in the creativity of advertising. But in spite of these purely advertising problems, if marketing itself were more disciplined in the creation of brands and in the use of consumer promotion, is it not possible that advertising could continue to make successful brands out of advertising whole cloth?

---

[1] Lambert, Gerard, *All Out of Step*, Doubleday & Company, Inc., Garden City, N.Y., 1956, p. 122.

[2] Marquis, Alice Goldfarb, *Hopes and Ashes*, Free Press, New York, 1986, p.122.

[3] Martin, David N., *Romancing the Brand*, AMACOM, New York, 1989, p. 19.

[4] Reeves, Rosser, *Reality in Advertising*, Alfred A. Knopf, New York, 1961, pp. 46–62.

[5] "New Alka-Seltzer Ads Revert to the Humor of Heartburn," *Wall Street Journal*, November 7, 1985, p. 31.

[6] "Alka-Seltzer Puts Humor Back in Ads," *New York Times*, January 26, 1990, p. D12.

[7] Higgins, Denis, *The Art of Writing Advertising*, NTC Business Books, Lincolnwood, IL, 1965, p. 43.

[8] Ailloni–Charas, Dan, *Promotion*, John Wiley & Sons, New York, 1984, p. 190.

[9] "Ford's Deep Pockets Are no Longer so Full," *New York Times*, January 9, 1991, p. D4.

[10] Tedlow, Richard S., *New and Improved*, Basic Books, New York, 1990, p. 367.

Chapter 7

Consumer Brand Loyalty Versus Brand Acceptance

Myth #5. Marketing activities make consumers loyal to brands.

One of the most insidious myths about how marketing works is that marketing causes brand loyalty. As the preceding discussion has suggested, many of the marketing forces that are supposed to cause brand loyalty seem to be, for one reason or another, increasingly ineffective.

The proliferation of brands that has occurred in product category after product category is seemingly at the root of the problem, since such proliferation destroys the very brand distinctiveness that must bring about brand loyalty. If the perceived differences among brands are not great, there is little or no reason for consumers to become loyal to particular brands.

However, as we shall see in this chapter, there is extensive evidence that brand loyalty has never been much of a factor in most package-goods product categories. And, unlike consumer durables, there is enough purchase frequency to at least provide conditions for significant levels of brand loyalty to develop.

ALTERNATIVE VIEWS ABOUT BRAND LOYALTY

As it turns out, there are alternative viewpoints about brand loyalty and its nature. On the one hand, as we have seen, marketers believe, almost as an article of faith, that brand loyalty is a permanent condition in most package goods markets. The reality and pervasiveness of brand loyalty in the marketplace, as marketers believe, is suggested in this typical view:

> Brand loyalty is not a matter of "what did you do for me today?" but stems from a kaleidoscope of impressions and experiences, from [product] form as well as function. Advertising reinforces these impressions to solidify the consumer base, convert infrequent users into frequent ones, and turn frequent users into single brand loyalists.[1]

This conception of brand loyalty implies a rational process in the consumer choice among brands. In such a process, the consumer is supposed to weigh consciously the pros and cons of alternative brands, after which a final decision is made about which brand is best. It is, then, this brand to which consumers become loyal.

Both intrinsic brand-performance characteristics and extrinsic advertising arguments are believed to facilitate this process, with the caveat that the brand itself must perform well enough that the promises of advertising are not contradicted by consumer experience.

There are a significant number of academic studies that seem to confirm the rational basis of consumer brand choice. As Richard Olshavsky and Donald Granbois observed during a review of academic research on consumer-purchase decision making:

> The most pervasive and influential assumption in consumer-behavior research is that purchases are preceded by a decision process.[2]

However, after reviewing most, if not all, academic studies available to them in 1979, Olshavsky and Granbois concluded that many of these studies did not, in fact, substantiate the view that consumer decisions are rational. As they put it:

> A significant portion of purchases may not be preceded by a decision process. This conclusion does not simply restate the familiar observation that purchase behavior rapidly becomes habitual, with little or no prepurchase

processes occurring after the first few purchases. We conclude that for many purchases a decision process never occurs, not even on the first purchase.[3]

There is certainly a good deal of intuitive sense in this conclusion— just what rational decision process can a consumer be expected to bring to bear on the array of ready-to-eat breakfast cereal brands that is presented in the retail environment pictured in Exhibit 7–1 or the array of toothpaste brands in the retail environment shown in Exhibit 7–2?

The Olshavsky and Granbois conclusion is not based on intuition but upon a comprehensive and hard-headed evaluation of academic research, at least as it was available to them in 1979.

But to say that rational decision making does not take place in many consumer purchase decisions does not say what does happen. Nor does it say what purchase situation stimuli or forces lead consumers to finally choose the brands that they do.

Given the Olshavsky and Granbois finding, it is not surprising that an alternative view of how consumers choose among brands, at least among package goods brands, has developed among some marketing theorists and marketing researchers. But, again not surprisingly, this alternative view has not found much acceptance among marketing practitioners or those academics who are firmly wedded to the rational theory of brand choice.

The key idea in this alternative viewpoint is that much consumer purchase behavior is *not* based on continuous, rational, and involved evaluation of alternative brands. Consumers are *not* continually reading labels, attending to the detail of advertisements, or evaluating product performance according to a set battery of criteria. Instead, consumers view the vast majority of their brand purchases as rather trivial events that do not require continuous or attentive decision making.

The tendency under these circumstances is for consumers to develop a group or set of brands that is acceptable and then to concentrate their purchases among this group or set of brands.

Casual exposure to advertising, package labels, and actual product performance may all play a part in the development of this acceptable set of brands. All of these may also influence the entrance of new brands into a particular consumer's acceptable set or the disappearance of previously acceptable brands from the set. But consumers may also learn of acceptable brands during their childhood and adolescence, or through interaction with others in social situations and in other cultural circumstances, or in any of a variety of other non-evaluative learning experiences.

EXHIBIT 7–1   Retail display of ready-to-eat cereal brands—1992

EXHIBIT 7–2   Retail display of toothpaste brands—1992

This does not mean that consumers are mere robots, randomly distributing their purchases among a group or set of relatively similar brands within each product category. What it does mean is that each consumer more or less informally settles upon a limited number of brands that that consumer personally believes to be acceptable. Thus, there is little or no continuing rational evaluation of brands in the purchase process. One of the acceptable brands may be chosen in preference to another because the consumer is simply seeking variety, or because of a coupon or a promotional price feature on the brand, or because one brand is the only acceptable brand that happens to be in stock, or whatever.

The point is that consumers do not think through every brand choice nor are they mostly loyal to a single brand as a result of such thought processes. They are perfectly satisfied with any of the brands from their acceptable set that happen to be available when the purchase is made.

This tendency to systematize relatively trivial, continuous decisions in brand purchases as well as in other daily activities is, as Sir Alfred North Whitehead reminds us, one of the hallmarks of our civilization:

> Civilization advances by extending the number of operations which we can perform without thinking about them.[4]

But this alternative point of view about the processes through which consumers make brand purchase decisions is not widely held by marketing practitioners. They believe, as we have seen above, that brand loyalty develops almost as a consequence of the rational way in which consumers choose among brands. It is not by chance that so much consumer advertising for brands depends upon rational argument.

But if one accepts the alternative, non-rational explanation of consumer brand choice, marketing should be at least as concerned with making brands acceptable—helping brands thus to gain entry into every consumer's set of acceptable brands—as in making the final conclusive, clinching sales argument that will win the consumer's loyalty forever.

Analyses based upon the alternative non-rational point of view about brand choice were, as it happens, not especially hard to find in the academic literature as early as 1969 and on into the 1970s.

For example, in a widely quoted remark, John Howard and Jagdish Sheth observed in 1969:

> The not-as-obvious point here is that the buyer does not choose among all of the available brands in the product class.... The brands that the buyer considers as acceptable for his next purchase constitute his *evoked set.*

The buyer simplifies his choice process by choosing from only among a few [brands].[5]

In 1976, Thomas Robertson stated:

A large share of consumption is trivial, unimportant, and non-ego-involving, such that beliefs and preferences are not strongly held and there is a lack of commitment to the purchase modality.[6]

Michael Rothschild commented in 1979:

Because the object class is not inherently involving, the consumer is more likely to make satisficing rather than optimizing decisions. Since decisions are made to be satisficing, any of several brands which lie in the evoked set and therefore merit minimum cutoff requirements would be adequate.[7]

It is at this point that the dialogue has more or less rested. Marketers believe that brand loyalty exists and believe that they are in the exacting business of creating it. This belief has been strengthened by the view widely held by academics that consumer brand choice is based on a rational process, and that the end product of such rational decision making is brand loyalty. A few academics are less certain that consumers care enough about brands to consciously and continuously analyze the differences among them or go to the trouble of becoming loyal to them.

Marketers tend to ignore academic views unless the academics agree with them. Thus, there has been little enthusiasm in the marketing community for any argument that brand loyalty is tenuous or even that it does not exist. And since the academic community has almost nothing to do with the day-to-day marketing of brands, what they think about how consumers make brand choices, rationally or otherwise, is, in any event, irrelevant to the practice of marketing.

THE EHRENBERG EVIDENCE

This debate between those who believe in rational brand choice and brand loyalty and those who believe in non-rational brand choice and weak or non-existent brand loyalty has pretty much ignored a very substantial body of evidence about how consumers choose among brands. As it happens, this evidence comes down decisively on the side of those who believe that most consumers do not forge decisive loyalties to brands, most of the time.

The work in question, which covers a period of almost thirty years, starting in the 1960s, is associated with the London Business School and especially with the originator of this work, statistician Andrew S.C. Ehrenberg. If one idea may be said to have illuminated Ehrenberg's work through the years, it is that, in studying consumer behavior, *the only important thing is what consumers actually do*. What marketing theorists or practitioners believe that consumers do, or speculate that consumers do, is, in Ehrenberg's view, irrelevant.

Ehrenberg's work has been concentrated primarily among consumer package-goods brands in more or less stable market situations, and it now covers well in excess of thirty product categories. The basic data that Ehrenberg works with come from consumer purchase panels—that is, from a sample of households that agree to report their brand *purchase* activities, usually in formal, product purchase diaries, from week to week and year to year. Ehrenberg has analyzed such product purchase data from a variety of countries including Great Britain, those of Western Europe, the United States, and Japan.

A major finding is that the basic patterns of consumer brand purchase in individual product categories do not vary much from category to category —that is, consumers tend to exhibit the same purchase-behavior patterns no matter what they are buying.

A second major finding is that the basic pattern of consumer purchases does not vary much from country to country—that is, consumers tend to follow the same purchase-behavior patterns no matter where they live, no matter what language they speak, and no matter what culture they are surrounded by. Ehrenberg's basic findings about consumer buying behavior, which often seem deceptively simple, can be summarized in five basic ideas.

1. Total Sales

Total sales for a brand are equal to the total number of consumers who buy the brand in a period of time multiplied by the number of occasions on which the brand is purchased, multiplied by the average number of units (by size of package) that are purchased on each purchase occasion.

> Thus, brand sales in a period = the number of customers × the number of purchase occasions × the number of units (by size of package) in the average purchase

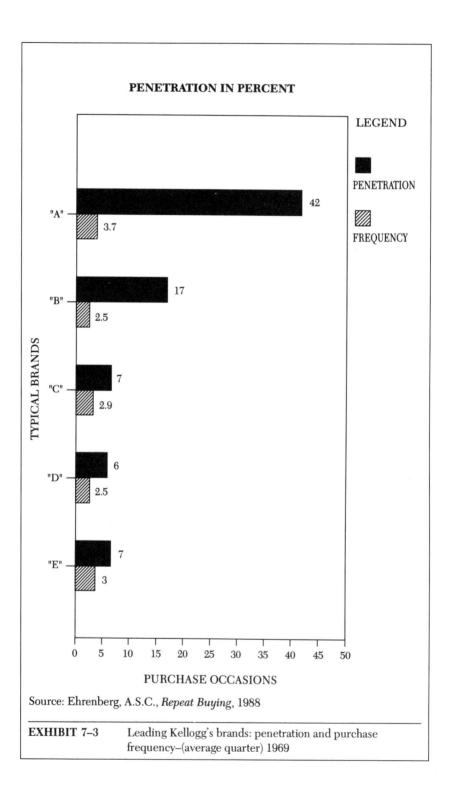

PENETRATION IN PERCENT

LEGEND

PENETRATION

FREQUENCY

TYPICAL BRANDS

"A" — 42 / 3.7

"B" — 17 / 2.5

"C" — 7 / 2.9

"D" — 6 / 2.5

"E" — 7 / 3

PURCHASE OCCASIONS

0 5 10 15 20 25 30 35 40 45 50

Source: Ehrenberg, A.S.C., *Repeat Buying*, 1988

EXHIBIT 7–3   Leading Kellogg's brands: penetration and purchase frequency–(average quarter) 1969

For example, Ehrenberg reported on a 1972 study of purchase patterns for the five leading brands of Kellogg's ready-to-eat cereals in the United Kingdom. In that study, brand "B"[8] was purchased by 17 percent of all households during a typical calendar quarter. The average consumer purchased brand "B" 2.5 times during the quarter, and the average purchase size was 1.03 packages.[9]

This is expressed as follows for the average quarter:

Brand "B" total purchases (purchase "penetration") = 17.0%

Brand "B" purchase occasions (purchase "frequency") = 2.5

Brand "B" purchases per purchase occasion = 1.03

If there are 1,000,000 households in the total population, total unit sales for a calendar quarter would be calculated as follows:

$1,000,000 \times .17 \times 2.5 \times 1.03 = 437,750$ units per quarter

2. Brand Penetration Versus Purchase Frequency

Brand penetration varies widely by brand, but purchase frequency does not.

The total number of consumers buying a brand in any period varies widely from brand to brand, but the average number of times it is purchased by consumers tends to be much more stable.

Exhibit 7–3 shows this for several typical brands in a single market. The penetration in a quarter varies from 42 percent (brand "A") to 6 percent (brand "D"), but brand purchase frequency hovers between 2.5 (brands "B" and "D") and 3. 7 (brand "A").

3. Purchase Frequency

Average purchase frequency tends to be constant from quarter to quarter.

Average brand purchase frequency stays relatively stable from quarter to quarter, as Exhibit 7–4 reveals.

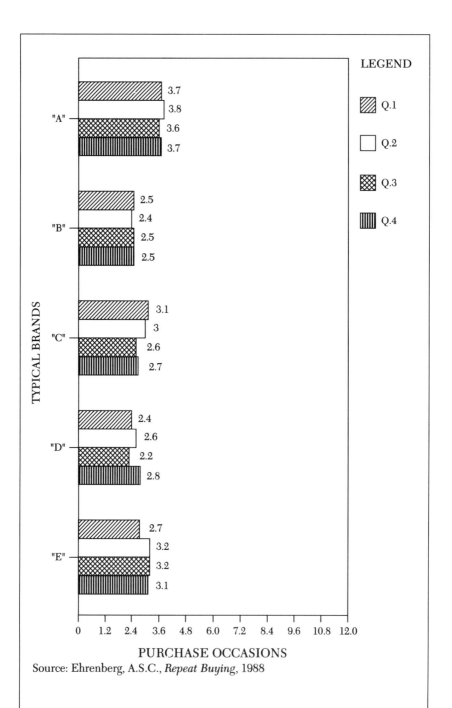

LEGEND

Q.1
Q.2
Q.3
Q.4

TYPICAL BRANDS

"A" 3.7 / 3.8 / 3.6 / 3.7

"B" 2.5 / 2.4 / 2.5 / 2.5

"C" 3.1 / 3 / 2.6 / 2.7

"D" 2.4 / 2.6 / 2.2 / 2.8

"E" 2.7 / 3.2 / 3.2 / 3.1

PURCHASE OCCASIONS

Source: Ehrenberg, A.S.C., *Repeat Buying*, 1988

EXHIBIT 7–4   Leading Kellogg's brands: purchase frequency—(quarter by quarter) 1969

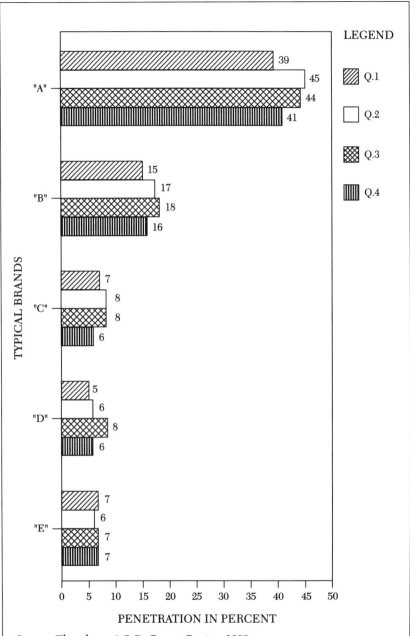

LEGEND

Q.1

Q.2

Q.3

Q.4

TYPICAL BRANDS

"A" — 39 / 45 / 44 / 41

"B" — 15 / 17 / 18 / 16

"C" — 7 / 8 / 8 / 6

"D" — 5 / 6 / 8 / 6

"E" — 7 / 6 / 7 / 7

0 5 10 15 20 25 30 35 40 45 50

PENETRATION IN PERCENT

Source: Ehrenberg, A.S.C., *Repeat Buying*, 1988

EXHIBIT 7–5   Leading Kellogg's brands: penetration—(quarter to quarter) 1969

4. Brand Penetration

Similarly, brand penetration does not change much for any given brand, from quarter to quarter.

The relative stability of individual brand penetration from quarter to quarter is shown in Exhibit 7–5.

5. Consumers' Brand Purchases

Consumers are not loyal to any one brand. Instead they distribute their purchases among several brands.

If the proportion of consumers who buy a brand remains relatively stable over time, and if each brand is purchased on about the same number of occasions in any period, does this mean that consumers are brand loyal? Do they purchase the same brand on almost every purchase occasion? That is, if 15 percent of all customers buy brand "B" in quarter 1 an average of 2.5 times, and if 17 percent of all consumers buy brand "B" in quarter 2 an average of 2.4 times, are these the same, or mostly the same customers, or are they different?

Ehrenberg's data indicate, overwhelmingly, that the same customers do *not* buy the same brand most of the time. Different groups of consumers tend to buy a brand in different time periods. Some of the buyers are the same from period to period; most of the buyers are usually different.

Thus, for example, Ehrenberg reports that buyers of brand "A" in a given calendar quarter satisfy 51 percent of their product category needs in any quarter with brand "A" and the remaining 49 percent with other brands. This 50–50 split of purchase between brand "A" and other brands is about as close to brand loyalty as the consumers who purchase any brand in this product category are likely to get.

As Exhibit 7–6 shows, for purchasers of brand "B" in a calendar quarter, 84 percent of their purchases in the product category are made of brands *other* than "B." Comparable percentages of total category purchases in *other* brands are 79 percent for purchasers of brand "C"; 74 percent for purchasers of brand "D"; and 71 percent for purchasers of brand "E."

The typical purchaser buys, in fact, an average of 1.7 different brands per quarter and an average of 2.5 different brands over a period of 48 weeks.

Further, consumers who have the most experience with the product category tend to buy more brands in any time period than consumers who are lighter purchasers. In Ehrenberg's analysis, light buyers of the product category (1 to 12 purchases in 48 weeks, 55 percent of total volume) bought

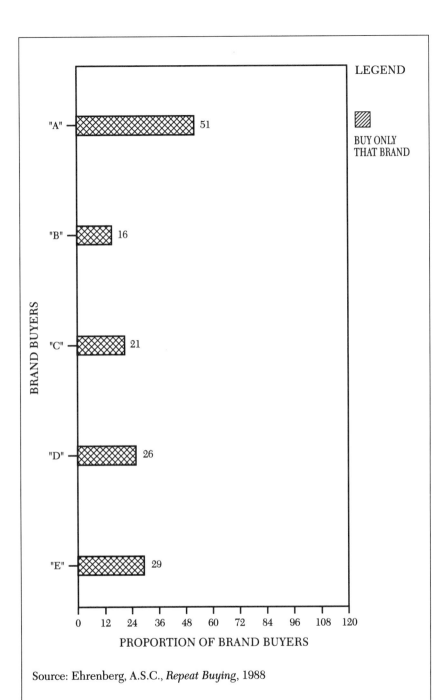

LEGEND

BUY ONLY
THAT BRAND

BRAND BUYERS

"A" 51

"B" 16

"C" 21

"D" 26

"E" 29

0 12 24 36 48 60 72 84 96 108 120

PROPORTION OF BRAND BUYERS

Source: Ehrenberg, A.S.C., *Repeat Buying*, 1988

EXHIBIT 7–6   Proportion of Kellogg's leading brand buyers who buy only that brand—(typical quarter) 1969

an average of 1.9 brands in 48 weeks; medium buyers (13–25 purchases, 25 percent of total volume) bought an average of 3.0 brands in 48 weeks; and heavy buyers (more than 26 purchases, 21 percent of total volume) bought an average of 3.6 different brands in 48 weeks.

It is important to note that, in this analysis, the number of brands in the category is only five. That is, the *maximum* number of brands that any consumer could purchase in any time period, under the ground rules in this analysis, is only five.[10]

As we have pointed out before, the fewer the brands there are in a product category, the greater the chance for brand differentiation and, thus, for brand loyalty. Conversely, the more brands in the category, the smaller the chance for meaningful brand differentiation and the less likelihood of any brand loyalty at all.

The same consumer purchase patterns are, in Ehrenberg's continuing analysis of more than 30 years, repeated for brand after brand in product category after product category. There is an ebb and flow of buyers, in and out of the brand's purchase group as time unfolds. Some buyers buy a particular brand more frequently than others, to be sure, but relatively few, if any, are *exclusive* or *very frequent* buyers of a particular brand in the product category.

Ehrenberg and Goodhart summarize this picture of low loyalty to individual brands as follows:

> In practice, any consumer's purchases tend to spread across some "repertoire" of brands with which he or she is familiar. This repertoire will vary from consumer to consumer; on average, it will match up with the brand's market share.[11]

The fact that consumer brand-purchase behavior has become systematized in this way does not mean that every consumer acts in exactly the same way, nor that all consumers have exactly the same repertoire of brands. Consumers' needs, experiences, and preferences do vary. They have different brand repertoires, and individual consumers may even be likely to have a weak preference, everything else being equal, for one brand rather than others.

What is important about all of this is its pervasiveness. By 1991, Ehrenberg and his colleagues had confirmed these general, consumer brand-purchase patterns in the following categories:

aviation fuels, biscuits, breakfast cereals, butter, canned vegetables, cat and dog foods, coffee, confectionery, convenience foods, cooking fats and oils, cosmetics, deodorants, detergents, disinfectants, disposable diapers, fabric softeners, feminine protection, flour, food drinks, frozen foods, gasoline, hairsprays, household soaps, household cleaners, instant potatoes, jams and jellies, margarine, motor oil, paper tissues, peanut butter spreads, polishes, processed cheese, refrigerated dough, sausages, shampoos, soft drinks, soup, take-home beer, toilet paper, toilet soap, toothpaste, TV programs, washing-up liquids.[12]

This list includes two non-consumer-goods products: aviation fuels and TV programs. Ehrenberg has extended his analysis to the purchase of aviation fuels by operators of airplanes and airlines. Although this has little to do with the point being made here, it does suggest the comprehensiveness of the behavior pattern that lies at the heart of his conclusions.

As far as television-program choice is concerned, his analysis of viewers' behavior has also been underway for over 25 years and reveals the same kinds of program choice behavior as summarized above for package-goods product choice.[13]

WHAT ABOUT SEGMENTED MARKETS?

If there is any significant amount of brand loyalty in any market, one would perhaps expect to find it within specific product segments in markets that have been calculatedly "segmented" by manufacturers. Thus, for example, in the toothpaste category one might expect to find loyalty within the "cavity prevention segment," or the "cosmetic segment," or the "breath-freshening segment," or whatever.

If such segmentation is itself valid, one would not expect to find a generally low loyalty to individual brands nor a more or less general substitution among brands, regardless of the segment within which they putatively fall. Yet, this is exactly what the Ehrenberg data reveal. As Exhibit 7–7 shows, buyers of any one brand of toothpaste are also likely to purchase other brands of toothpaste, more or less indiscriminately, during a 52 week period.

	Buyers of				
	Colgate GRF	Aqua-fresh	Crest R&FM	Macleans Fresh	Ultra brite
Percent who bought:	%	%	%	%	%
Colgate GRF	–	19	18	20	15
Aqua–fresh	30	–	26	28	25
Crest R&FM	32	28	–	23	21
Macleans Fresh	31	27	20	–	29
Metadent P	28	21	22	18	17
Colgate Gel	53	24	23	23	19
Signal	34	34	23	27	24
Gibbs SR	37	28	19	27	21
Macleans Mild	34	27	24	44	22
Ultra brite	34	35	27	30	–
Sensodyne	24	14	16	18	6
Colgate GRF Dispenser	54	19	15	19	11
Colgate Gel Dispenser	31	17	17	19	12

Source: Data supplied by A.S.C. Ehrenberg, 1991

EXHIBIT 7–7   Brand purchase duplication: toothpaste purchasers in the United Kingdom—Twelve months of 1985

As Ehrenberg and Goodhart generalize about segmented marketing:

With new brands, marketing people often start with the idea that it must be different to succeed. They therefore try to establish some consumer need which differentiates a sizeable sub-group of consumers from the rest (e.g., saying that they prefer the product pinker or less perfumed or whatever). A new brand with the required characteristics is then launched at this segment.

Most members of the target group may be attracted by the new brand—it offers them something which the research (if valid) indicated is important to them. But this attraction is unlikely to be overwhelming or exclusive in terms of brand choice. The evidence of buyer behavior is that they have already been buying brands which do *not* have that special property, and also that they will go on buying them.[14]

What Ehrenberg seems to have discovered is an innate pattern of consumer behavior. The basic patterns of such behavior were well-established by the late 1960s, particularly for consumers in Great Britain. But they have now been generalized to other countries and other cultures. The rule of brand repertoire formation as a basis of brand purchase behavior appears to be pervasive. Strict brand loyalty in a product category—to the extent that it exists at all—is the exception, not the rule.

This innate behavior pattern—the formation of brand repertoires as a basis of brand purchase behavior—does not mean that marketing efforts in behalf of a brand cannot be successful. What it does mean is that marketing success does not come about as a result of the development of brand loyalty. Rather, marketing success depends upon two rather different accomplishments:

■ The development of brands that win widespread consumer trial, especially when first developed. As we have seen, relatively great market penetration does not come about as a result of brand loyalty, but it obviously can come about as a result of marketing activities and, particularly, those marketing activities that support and win wide trial for the new brand during its introductory period. The more valuable a brand is made to seem to consumers, the greater its initial trial is likely to be.

■ The development of brand *acceptability* on the broadest possible scale should have highest marketing priority. Acceptability does not mean decisive preference, it means brand repertoire membership. As Ehrenberg's data imply, the more consumer repertoires a brand is found in, the higher its market share is likely to be. The goal of marketing activities is not necessarily to convince consumers of brand superiority but, rather, to make the brand at least minimally acceptable to as many consumers as possible. The more valuable a brand is made to seem to consumers, the more acceptable it is likely to be, and the more brand repertoires it is likely to join.

The history of marketing, as portrayed by Ehrenberg's data, suggests that brands do not come to be perceived by consumers as unique, but rather as widely interchangeable, no matter what marketing efforts have been expended to differentiate them.

Most of Ehrenberg's basic analysis and its conclusions were known by the early 1970s. The innate consumer-behavior patterns described above had developed well *before* the explosive proliferation of brands in the 1980s.

The proliferation of brands has not *caused* a decline in brand loyalty, for there was never a lot of brand loyalty to begin with. But certainly, the availability of more brands and more undifferentiated brands in the past few years has reinforced the innate consumer behavior patterns that Ehrenberg first identified some thirty years ago.

If brand loyalty has not been much of a factor in consumer behavior, the mindless proliferation of brands must render marketing initiatives increasingly ineffective.

To put the point in a different way: There is little hope that consumers will ever find a brand or brand variant acceptable, let alone become loyal to it, unless that brand or brand variant has some sort of decisive value—either real or illusory—for that consumer.

[1] Martin, David N., *Romancing the Brand*, AMACOM, New York, 1989, pp. xiv–xv.

[2] Olshavsky, Richard W., and Donald H. Granbois, "Consumer Decision Making—Fact or Fiction?" *Journal of Consumer Research*, Vol. 6, September, 1979, p. 93.

[3] Ibid., p. 98.

[4] Whitehead, Sir Alfred North, quoted in Medawar, Sir Peter, *Pluto's Republic*, Oxford University Press, New York, 1982, p. 195.

[5] Howard, John A., and Jagdish N. Sheth, *The Theory of Buyer Behavior*, John Wiley & Sons, Inc., New York, 1969, pp. 98–99.

[6] Robertson, Thomas S., "Low-Commitment Consumer Behavior," *Journal of Advertising Research*, 16:2, April, 1976, p. 22.

[7] Rothschild, Michael L., "Advertising Strategies from High and Low Involvement Situations," J.C. Maloney and B. Silverman (Eds.), *Attitude Research Plays for High Stakes*, American Marketing Association, Chicago, 1979, p. 84.

[8] In Ehrenberg's narrative example, the identity of all brands are coded out in accordance with his agreement with data suppliers. The underlying data are, of course, real.

[9] Ehrenberg, A.S.C., *Repeat Buying*, Oxford University Press, New York, 1988, pp. 33, 36, 39.

[10] Ibid., p. 176.

[11] Ehrenberg, A.S.C., and C. J. Goodhart, *Understanding Buyer Behavior: Market Segmentation*, J. Walter Thompson Company, New York, 1978, p. 4.10.

[12] List supplied to the author by Andrew Ehrenberg in 1991.

[13] Barwise, Patrick, and Andrew Ehrenberg, *Television and Its Audience*, Sage Publications, Newbury Park, CA, 1988.

(The Barwise/Ehrenberg findings about television viewing will not surprise marketers who have studied the audience coverage and frequency of viewing patterns revealed by the A. C. Nielsen data in the United States.)

[14] Ehrenberg, A.S.C., and C. J. Goodhart, *Understanding Buyer Behavior: Market Segmentation*, J. Walter Thompson Company, New York, 1978, p. 4.10.

I AM THE VERY MODEL
OF A MANAGER
OF MARKETING

By Tracy Carlson

I am the very model of a manager of marketing
With demonstrated mastery of mass consumer targeting.
From durable to wearable or blandest of the branded goods
I've vaulted to the leadership of this exalted band of hoods.

A decorated vet'ran of the burger, beer and cola wars,
I've launched a hundred products which the public on the whole adores.
Of strategems and ruses I've a marvelous sufficiency,
Selected from my arsenal, deployed with true efficiency.

I handle every segment, niche and demo with felicity.
I'm handy with an ethnic pitch, an expert at publicity.
In short, for all the latest trends in mass consumer targeting
I am the very model of a manager of marketing.

If ScanTrack shows a district has a market share emergency,
I'll shore it up with FSI's and gimmicks point-of-purchasy.
If reading purchase data I detect a demographic skew,
I'll write a snappy questionnaire and find some folks to ask it to.

Should R&D's new formula bedevil Manufacturing,
I'll have the same old product put in new and fancy packaging.
Should market checks reveal our facings dropped to just a minimum,
I'll roll some line extensions out in herbal, mint and cinnamon.

When parity positioning inspires only tedium,
I'll tweak the mix with upscale graphics, pricing at a premium.
For all the latest, greatest trends in mass consumer targeting,
I am the very model of a manager of marketing.

Though lavishly I'm entertained through Agency extravagance,
I'll cheerfully dismember a production bid with half a glance.
If new creative gives the brand a touch of added piquancy,
I'll run it in a heavy-up, augmenting reach and frequency.

My artistry is getting you to siphon off your salaries
On basic needs like Hula-Hoops, fast cars and empty calories.
From aloe-mist deodorant to mousse or chocolate cereal,
If profits can be made from it, the product's immaterial.

No matter if the goods should be outlandish or impractical,
I'll grab with the strategic hook and pummel with the tactical.
For profitable mastery of mass consumer targeting
I am the very model of a manager of marketing.

Chapter 8

Corporate Culture and Contemporary Marketing Practice

Marketing preaches distinctive brands. In contemporary marketing practice, however, the dominant activity is the multiplication of brands and brand variants with inconsequential differences.

Previous chapters have suggested that brand proliferation tends to come about as a result of forces that the corporation cannot control—the intransigence of the trade; the long-term decline in advertising creativity; the fact that consumers usually do not become loyal to brands no matter what marketers do to make them so.

Of course, the corporation and only the corporation is reponsible for the character and quality of the brands and brand variants that it markets to the public. And, as we have seen, there are basic pressures and misconceptions in the process of new product and brand development that tend to lead even the well-meaning corporation to proliferate brands with meaningless differences.

But there is more to the corporation's proliferation of meaningless brands than ineptness and wrong-headedness in the product/brand/brand variant development process itself. A basic cause is the ways corporations organize themselves to market their brands.

It may be reasonable enough to assume that corporations are only interested in the creation and maintenance of dominant and profitable brands based upon consumer value and competitive excellence. However, the reality is that the imperatives that corporations adopt for their businesses and the organizational forms that they impose upon themselves make a significant contribution to the uncontrolled proliferation of brands.

CORPORATE IMPERATIVES AND THE PROLIFERATION OF BRANDS

One of the truisms of business is that the internal policies of corporations tend to force their organizations in the direction of commodity marketing. Thus, what corporations do—as opposed to what they say they do or what they wish to do—forces their employees to eschew the innovative, avoid radical change, and continuously follow the path of lowest risk. Unhappily, the path of lowest risk is almost always the path of least reward. What are these corporate imperatives that guarantee minimal risk and minimal rewards?

The Diffusion of Risk

A guiding principle of business is to diffuse rather than concentrate risk. Thus, the surest, safest way to increase sales and profits is to elaborate brands and brand variants, expanding the scope of each to gain—it is hoped —sales away from competitors. Even if some of the sales that come from such segmenting of markets and extending of brands derive from the corporation's existing brands and brand variants, the plan and the hope is always that there will be a net gain in total, and that the new brand and brand variants will create enough new sales at the expense of competition to justify themselves.

The alternative, of course, is to concentrate corporate resources against a limited number of brands and brand variants that are consciously designed to be superior to competitive brands. Such a strategy commits the corporation to the continuing pursuit of competitive brand excellence and decisive consumer value. Sales are achieved by frontal assault upon competitors rather than by a series of minor moves calculated only to cadge a sales dollar here, a sales dollar there, either through the development of minimal product differences or by matching the competitors' product line, brand by brand and brand variant by brand variant.

The argument against the concentrated pursuit of competitive excellence is twofold:

- First is the argument that the market itself has changed and that it can now only be satisfied by the continuing fragmentation of established brands through the development of their segmenters and extenders. But if this is so, does it not mean that the pursuit of excellence is impossible?

- The second response is that knowledge of and competence in technology is now so widespread that it is impossible to achieve competitive excellence in most consumer-goods categories through dependence upon either innovative technology or manufacturing practice. But if this is so, why talk about product differences at all, and why spend so much money on research and development?

Is it not the purpose of the corporation to seek and achieve competitive advantage through innovation? If this is impossible, best to admit it straight out rather than grinding out products without distinction while asserting that they are different.

In the end, most corporations avoid risk. They do this by diffusing it through the ongoing development of a variety of products that have neither the potential for serious gain nor, more important, the potential for serious loss.

The Diffusion of Corporate Focus

In too many corporations the brand has become an end of corporate activity in and of itself. Each brand is treated as a separate planning center and as a separate profit center. The corporation becomes, thus, the sum of all its brands. The corporation neither thinks nor acts as a monolith with a single central purpose, other than the accumulation of profits across the individual brands.

If each of the brands "makes the number," all will be well. The individual brand will then be permitted to continue along, unhampered by central direction, in happy pursuit of its "numbers."

There is nothing much to do, in all of this, with the consumer and how the consumer may best be served. Nor is there anything much to do with the role of the individual brand in achieving those goals of the corporation that do not focus upon immediate profit. The individual brand justifies itself with continued modest growth and assured profit contribution according to the corporation's institutionalized financial-planning processes.

From time to time, to be sure, the brand may be enriched or revitalized by some sort of contribution from R&D. But there is equal, if not greater, pressure back from each brand to R&D, to assure that the brand maintains pace with the marketplace and the accomplishments of its competitors. The preoccupation is with the maintenance of competitive equilibrium since such equilibrium is certain to perpetuate the brand's sales and profits, no matter what R&D may, eventually, come up with.

Aggressive marketing is replaced by a marketing stasis in which the marketing thrust of any given brand tends to be exactly offset by the collective marketing thrusts of competitive brands. This may not be what marketers yearn for in their heart of hearts, but it is what they know, in their mind of minds, will satisfy the financial goals of the corporation. Marketing stasis exists because corporations act in ways that ensure that stasis will exist and be perpetuated.

Corporate Innovation Is Divorced from Brand Management

The net effect of all this is to separate the future of the corporation from the corporation's brands. The existing brands provide the continuing income that permits the corporation to cast about for new opportunities and new worlds to conquer. But, too frequently, this corporate initiative is focused beyond the brands themselves—their destiny is left in the hands of the brand management system. It is the responsibility of this system to develop the predictable flow of sales and profits that will sustain the future of the corporation.

This fundamental separation between the business as it exists and the business as it will be in the future reflects an indifference to the fundamental consumer satisfaction that the products of the corporation should provide. It substitutes, in its place, other corporate prerogatives, usually financial. The corporation understands only that it is in the business of setting and meeting financial goals. It forgets that the brands of the corporation, and only its brands, will ultimately permit the corporation to meet its current financial obligations and accomplish its future expansion.

What is missing in all of this is a corporate commitment to a continuing competitive disequilibrium in the markets in which the corporation is active. Only such a commitment to market disequilibrium will, if it plays itself out successfully, generate new brands and products that will provide consumers with decisive value, gain competitive advantage, and, thus, gain incremental consumer allegiance.

Creating conditions of market disequilibrium in the long-term service of the consumer does not, in and of itself, guarantee a smooth flow of profits from quarter to quarter. What it does do, however, is to commit the corporation to the policy of controlling markets through the development of dominant and single-minded brands. In this conception, the brand is an entity whose only purpose is to create decisive consumer value because it is *better than its competitors*. Such brands are not a loose collection of market segmenters and line extenders created to maintain competitive equilibrium rather than competitive disruption.

This corporate unwillingness to create market disequilibrium and continuing competitive advantage is sustained by the brand management system as it has been developed and refined in the 1970s and 1980s.

THE BRAND MANAGEMENT SYSTEM AND THE PROLIFERATION OF BRANDS

The brand management system got its start over 60 years ago in a few forward-looking consumer package-goods companies–P&G and General Foods are most often cited in this connection.

P&G has described its brand management system in a company brochure as follows:

> Brand management is the mainspring and moving force behind all our consumer marketing. The brand management concept assures that each brand will have behind it the kind of single-minded drive it needs to succeed. ... The brand group is expected to know more about its product and how to increase its consumer acceptance than anyone else in the organization.[1]

In consumer package-goods companies in those days—the 1930s and 1940s—a set of relatively unique circumstances prevailed. No company had more than a handful of prosperous brands—10 or 15 at the most. Each was distinctive and unitary; there was little or no brand proliferation; and the concepts of market segmentation and line extension were still far in the future. Thus, these few brands dominated the corporate attention and formed a context within which the future of the corporation itself could be plotted.

Almost always, the brands themselves, taken together, defined an area of corporate competence and corporate commitment to the consumer. Brands would be added to the corporate roster only if they were consistent with this competence and commitment, and only if it was clear that they had the capacity to extend the web of consumer satisfaction that had been established by their brand predecessors in the corporation.

In this context the brand manager emerged as the guardian of the brand, its champion in the interest of the consumer, and its advocate within the corporation. The position of the brand manager gave corporate management relief from the day-to-day demands of the myriad brand-specific decisions about advertising, packaging, pricing, product refinement and improvement, and consumer and trade promotion. The brand manager also became responsible for the orderly flow of profits from the brand without the daily, hands-on attention of corporate management.

Corporate management was then free to pursue and extend the policies that had created this covey of successful brands and to continue to develop the consumer satisfaction that these policies had also created.

The single most important characteristic of these early brand-management systems was that some single person was responsible for both the profitability and the *destiny* of the brand. This person—perhaps with an assistant, perhaps not—and only this person, answered for the brand to corporate management. But corporate management did not relinquish nor delegate its own inherent interest in the fundamental well-being of the brand. More often than not, individuals within the corporate management had been intimately involved in the development and initial success of one or more of the individual corporate brands, and their residual interest in the brand was bound to be high.

BRAND MANAGEMENT TODAY

The brand management system has, as one would expect, evolved as the corporation itself has evolved. Perhaps the most noticeable characteristic of brand management in the typical corporation is that the function has become diffuse and hierarchical. In the early days, there was a single person, *the* brand manager who was responsible for *the* brand. Now the responsibility has become spread among several people with titles like vice president, marketing; group brand manager; senior brand manager; brand manager; associate brand manager; assistant brand manager; and so forth.

This hierarchical arrangement in the management of brands reflects a kind of general bureaucratization that has occurred throughout business, as businesses have grown and prospered in the past 50 years or so. As far as brand management is concerned, these hierarchical organizations have several implications.

The Final Objective

The final objective of hierarchical brand management is to prevent brand management mistakes.

The way the hierarchy typically works is for the development of new ideas or proposals for new actions to work their way from the bottom to the top of the hierarchy. New ideas or proposals are initiated at the top or, less frequently, further down the line, but they are developed and refined initially at the lowest hierarchical level. Documentation and support for the idea or proposal then moves up through the hierarchy, with objections or questions resolved at every level. The idea or proposal is continuously recycling, emerging finally for approval by the vice president of marketing or even by corporate management.

The hierarchical approach to brand management ensures that no marketing decision will *ever* be made in the absence of extensive critical review and documentation. The end result of such a system is, of course, blandness. Individual ideas and proposals are smoothed and refined until everyone in the hierarchy is satisfied. Ideas and proposals are developed not to strengthen their intrinsic merit, but to respond to anticipated reactions of others further up the hierarchy. Independent thought, even if it is present, is finally reduced to vanilla ice cream. In the end, this process provides not brand management in its classic sense, but brand direction by spineless consensus.

Individual Responsibility

The hierarchy ensures the absence of individual responsibility.

As the hierarchy performs its work, it is virtually certain that no individual will be solely responsible for any marketing decision. Many people in the organization have the right and authority to say "no" to a new marketing idea or proposal. But no one has the unequivocal right to say "yes." Every decision is a participative one. Every person in the marketing hierarchy will have had the opportunity to leave a mark on each marketing decision. Thus, everyone in the hierarchy can claim at least some credit for individual marketing successes—such as they may be—but no one can ever be solely blamed for marketing failures.

Although the brand manager is still supposed to be the champion of the consumer interest in the brand and its advocate within the corporation, in fact the brand manager emerges as a kind of absentee owner, with little or no power to decide or act.

The Work of the Brand Manager

But if the brand manager is no longer the consumer's champion nor the brand's advocate, what is the brand manager *really* supposed to do? Over the years, the real work of the brand manager has gradually, yet decisively, shifted away from championship and advocacy to a preoccupation with the financial performance of the brand, no more and no less.

This shift was vividly portrayed to readers of the *Harvard Business Review* as early as 1975:

> The strength of the [brand] manager concept of organization lies in the fact that it provides for a managerial focus on products or brands as profit generating systems.[2]

Somehow or other, the brand management system had grown away from its fundamental concern with the satisfaction of the consumer and the creation of decisive consumer value.

The Role of the Brand Manager

In the rhetoric of the corporation, however, the brand managers appear to be much more important than they are in reality. Brand managers are on the "fast" career track within the corporation. They expect to be promoted promptly up the marketing hierarchy and, perhaps, beyond, into the upper echelons of corporate management. This will happen, however, only if the brands to which they are assigned prosper or are perceived to have been well managed during the brand manager's tenure.

Thus, the brand manager is obliged to find ways to demonstrate capability and competence. The manager must leave some mark on the brand during tenure with it. In some companies, this mark must be found in brand success itself—goals must be met, market share or sales and profits must grow. In other firms, "making the numbers" is less important than the quality of the brand manager's performance. The brand manager is, thus, in these latter firms, evaluated in terms of initiatives in behalf of the brand and an ability to flourish as a personality within the corporate environment.

In choosing among actions that the brand manager can take to leave an indelible mark upon a brand, it is important to keep in mind the time frames that the brand manager must deal with. There are two of these: the financial time frame and the career time frame.

The financial time frame determines when the financial performance of the brand will be assessed. Financial performance is usually monitored on a quarterly basis and evaluated at least annually and often more frequently. The implication for the brand manager is that improvements in brand sales and profits must be continuous. But real breakthroughs are not necessary. It is enough to exceed the gradually escalating goals that have been established by financial management for the brand, usually at the beginning of each year.

The career time frame determines the length of time an individual brand manager may expect to be assigned to a particular brand. The length of assignment is normally 18 months, sometimes less, but rarely longer. The implication for the brand manager is that whatever projects are initiated during the career time that is dedicated to a single brand, they must be finished up before reassignment to another brand. If such initiatives are not completed within this time, their financial impact, if any, will inevitably accrue to the benefit of the successor brand manager.

It is within these time frames—financial and career—that the brand manager must appear to be making something happen to the assigned brand.

In addition, there are a number of busywork brand-marketing matters that must concern the brand manager during tenure with the brand. Thus, the brand manager will be concerned with modifications in advertising copy; with shifts in the expenditure patterns for media funds; with the evolution of package designs; with the resolution of cost-of-goods changes and their effect on brand pricing; with the administration of brand budgets; and so forth.

None of these busywork activities provides *any* immediate prospect for increases in brand sales or brand profitability. Thus, the *real* preoccupation of the brand manager must be with two areas of marketing activity that will almost certainly have an immediate impact upon brand sales: new brand variants and sales promotion. Changes in the advertising content can also be made, but if they are in any sense profound, they are likely to induce a considerable amount of discussion in the hierarchy. In any event, the effects of changes in advertising on sales are far from predictable.

Creating brand variants

In the case of brand variants, the brand manager's attention will almost inevitably be focused on those new expressions of the brand that will be easy to manufacture and that will either logically segment the existing market or extend the brand into areas that will either meet competition or outwit it. Only those brand variants will be considered that can be developed quickly and that are so logical, in the context of the brand as it now exists, that they will gain ready acceptance, up and down the hierarchy.

It should also be added that, even if the brand variants that the brand manager advocates are never introduced into the market, the mere fact that the brand manager advocates them will win recognition and approval. New brand variant development is, after all, what a brand manager is expected to do, and a vigorous program advocating new brand variants, as long as it is prudent, inexpensive to implement, and apparently well-founded, must help the brand manager's career.

The trick of brand-variant advocacy within the hierarchy is, of course, to choose those brand variations that have, at least, some sales potential; that do not poach upon the sales territory of sibling brands in the corporate-brand lineup; that do not violate any corporate strategy that may be relevant; and that are so inherently unobjectionable that the hierarchy will be hard pressed to either criticize them or require them to be recycled, up and down the hierarchy, to achieve consensus.

An especially pernicious practice in the manipulation of brands and brand variants is the attempt to reduce the cost of producing existing brands and brand variants. This is done by manipulating the formulation of the product to include lower cost ingredients or by modifying its structural characteristics to make it cheaper to produce. The net result of such brand manipulation is to make the brand more profitable, even as the brand itself is almost certainly made marginally less acceptable to some people who have previously regarded it as an acceptable alternative within the product class.

Generating sales with promotional mirrors

A second and even more attractive means to generate sales increases is through the use of either consumer or trade promotion.

The trade expects promotional price concessions, as we have seen in Chapter 4, to stock brands and to provide them with favored treatment within the retail environment. The more tenuous the brand, the greater the concessions that the trade is likely to seek. No one doubts, when the trade accepts such promotional payments, that the promotional merchandise will move out of the stores, and the richer the promotional stimulus, the faster the merchandise will move.

Alternatively, or concurrently, the brand may be promoted to the consumer, usually with price-off coupons, but also with promotional packs of one kind or another; manufacturer's rebates; consumer contests; consumer sweepstakes; or whatever. Again, the effect of the promotion will be felt on sales, and the more generous the promotion, the more widespread and decisive its impact upon sales.

As Dewar and Schultz put it:

> Need to make a quick splash in market share or sales volume? Promote! Product managers ... may have taken a while to catch on but now widely practice the oldest technique in the sales book. If you want to move the product, cut the price.[3]

Promotions, everyone agrees, do create sales increases in the short term, but what is the long-term impact of such activities upon the brand?

Some enthusiasts of promotion say that there is every reason to expect that promotions will have a long-term, positive effect upon brand sales. The argument is based upon the supposition that at least some, if not a great deal, of the merchandise that is sold as a result of promotion ends up in the hands of consumers who have had little or no previous experience of the brand. Thus, it is argued, promotions cause a desirable amount of sampling among brand prospects who have not previously been users. Such consumers will now have the opportunity to experience the virtues of the promoted brand and will be able to compare and contrast it to the brand or brands that they have previously judged to be satisfactory.

Automobile manufacturers believe that this same kind of sampling experience is available to car renters and, thus, are particularly anxious to make sales to the proprietors of car rental fleets. Renters who have had neither previous nor recent experience with a Ford or a Pontiac or a Dodge will, it is hoped, see these autos in a new and favorable light and remember the rental experience when they shop for their next new car.

The "promotional sampling leading to brand switching" argument tends to break down for two reasons. First of all, if the sampled product has no distinguishing characteristics, what can be gained by giving the consumer an opportunity to sample it? In the second place, and this is particularly true in the case of consumer package goods, most of the consumers who purchase the promoted brand have already categorized it as an *acceptable* brand in the category. (This would also be true for automobiles if car renters only rent brands that they have already determined to be acceptable.)

Indeed, there is abundant evidence, at least in package-goods product categories, that promotional events do not lead to any *long-term* sales gains. In fact, because so much merchandise that is purchased as a result of a promotion ends up in the hands of consumers who already consider the promoted brand to be at least acceptable and are willing to stockpile it at a promotional price, a promotion in one period is often followed by *lower than expected* sales in the period that follows the promotion. Thus, at least some promotions mortgage future sales by encouraging consumer stockpiling of promoted merchandise.

Most of our knowledge about the sales effects of specific promotions comes from the A.C. Nielsen Company. The way in which promotions work in package-goods categories had been well documented by the Nielsen Company at least as early as the late 1970s. Thus, the promotional effects that we are describing are traditional and have not been caused just by brand proliferation.

The late James Peckham, a long-term Nielsen executive, summarized his extensive experience in evaluating the effects of consumer price promotions on established package-goods brands:

... It has been fairly well documented that consumer price promotions generally do not affect the basic trend of the particular brand in question. The consumer sales effect is limited to the time period of the promotion itself. ...[4]

It is important to emphasize that most promotions apparently cause no residual sales effect—nothing happens, that is, except an increase in sales at off-price during the period in which the off-price merchandise is available, often followed by an offsetting post-promotion sales decline. Promotions do not increase subsequent brand sales.

If this lack of residual sales effect has not been caused by the proliferation of brands, the emergence of a good deal of brand proliferation certainly cannot be expected to change the pattern. In the first place, the proliferation of brands and brand variants and the popularity of promotions with brand managers can only mean that brand proliferation must lead inexorably, as it has, to promotion proliferation. The proliferation of brands is likely to make promotions even less effective. This happens because the more brands there are the more likely it is that promotional effects will be concentrated on those consumers who have already accepted the promoted brand as either equivalent to or a reasonable substitute for other brands in the consumer's existing product-category repertoire. And, even if a brand promotion does cause some consumer sampling, an undifferentiated brand purchased as a result of a promotion can offer the consumer little performance-based incentive to make futher purchases.

One final aspect of promotions—trade and consumer—remains to be investigated. About all that we have concluded about promotions so far is that they cause a short-term, off-price sales increase that does not continue after the promotion expires and the promotional merchandise returns to normal price. But this is enough for brand managers who are likely to argue that they are perfectly willing to take a predictable sales increase at less than normal margins, especially when the funds to cover the margin shortfall are available and budgeted.

The question then becomes: Just how cost effective are promotions? Are they *so* cost effective that they are the preferred method of dispersing marketing funds? John Philip Jones has addressed this question in an elegantly reasoned article in the *Harvard Business Review*. With regard to the short-term economic impact of promotions, Jones concludes:

> Indeed, it seems clear that in most circumstances, manufacturers that promote heavily are deliberately exchanging profit for volume: in other words, making less profit on more sales; or, to make the point more crudely, slicing into their own margins in dumping their merchandise.[5]

No matter what the arguments, pro or con, about promotions, the bottom line is that they have been developed to offer consumers an incentive—almost always price—to buy products that do not have enough inherent distinctiveness to appeal to the consumer *without* some extra incentive. The very nature of the incentive is to neutralize the consumer allegiance, if any, that the brand's previous marketing activities have created, by using an offsetting price concession. Of course, the less distinctive the product, the more important promotion becomes to it.

In fact, the promoted product is likely to be relatively unattractive to a consumer unless it is promoted, *if* there are products that offer superior value available in the marketplace. But, if all products are perceived by consumers to be more or less the same, price becomes the determining factor in purchase.

BRAND-MANAGEMENT CAREERS

In the end, the brand manager is forced by the brand-management system to pay more attention to career management than to brand management. Brand championship and brand advocacy are replaced by actions that make the brand manager look good to management, no matter what the long-term effect upon the brand or the perceptions of the consumers who buy it.

This curious set of circumstances has two additional implications that tend to reinforce, even further, the fundamental tendency of the corporation to encourage brand proliferation rather than competitive excellence.

First, no matter how fast a track the corporation establishes for the development of brand-management careers, the system itself offers no easy opportunities for brand managers to distinguish themselves either as genuine innovators in, nor as ultimate guardians of, the futures of their brands. This is both a function of the time that is allotted to each brand–brand manager relationship and a function of the realistically trivial responsibilities that the brand manager is given within the corporate marketing hierarchy.

The end result of these processes is that one brand manager tends to become indistinguishable from any other. Just as the brands they manage tend to become commodities, so too do their managers. Brand managers all relate to the marketing hierarchy in the same way: they all indulge in a good deal of superficial busywork in the management of their brands, and they all develop indistinguishable brand variants and humdrum promotional programs to propel their careers upward.

Perhaps even more insidious is the fact that the very young people who are meticulously chosen as the fast-track future leaders of their corporation's marketing efforts, or even of the corporation itself, are put in a work–learning environment that teaches them that superficial results linked to insistent short-term, financial-performance goals are what the success of the corporation is all about.

The future of corporations cannot depend upon consensus seeking and reactive brand managers, nor upon an environment that is almost always hostile to innovation, market disequilibrium, and the pursuit of decisive consumer value.

In the end it is not the brand managers who fail their corporations. Instead the problem is the other way round—it is the corporations who fail the brand managers by creating corporate imperatives and environments that permit the brand manager to prosper but not to grow.

And in the process the corporation itself provides the final dimension of the problem of contemporary marketing. No matter how difficult it is to operate in a marketing environment in which retailers are avaricious, advertising ineffective, and consumers indifferent, the corporation itself still has the opportunity—some would say the responsibility—to impose its will upon its marketing destiny. The evolution of the brand manager and the brand-management system clearly suggests that the corporation is relatively indifferent to what it does in the marketplace, as long as the quarterly financial returns move inexorably and predictably upwards.

---

[1] Quoted in: Schisgall, Oscar, *Eyes Upon Tomorrow*, Ferguson Publishing Company, Chicago, 1981, p. 163.

[2] Reprinted by permission of *Harvard Business Review*. "Shifting Roles of the Product Manager," by Richard M. Clewett and Stanley F. Stasch (January/February 1976). Copyright © 1976 by the President and Fellows of Harvard College, all rights reserved.

[3] Dewar, Robert, and Don Schultz, *The Product Manager: An Idea Whose Time Has Gone— Fast Track or Dead End?* Northwestern University, Evanston, IL, 1988, p. 13.

[4] Peckham, James O., *The Wheel of Marketing*, privately published, Scarsdale, NY, 1981, p. 69.

[5] Reprinted by permission of *Harvard Business Review*. "The Double Jeopardy of Sales Promotions," by John Philip Jones (September/October 1990). Copyright © 1990 by the President and Fellows of Harvard College, all rights reserved.

PART TWO

CREATING DECISIVE NEW CONSUMER VALUE FOR TODAY'S CONSUMERS

The dilemma of marketing can only finally be resolved through a corporate determination to create decisive consumer value.

This requires the development of marketing strategies that will create value, real or illusory, that consumers will perceive to be decisive in their choice of products and brands.

Chapter 9

Integrated Marketing

> Marketing must be thought of as an integrated whole—
> not as a loose collection of uncoordinated acts.

If the problems of contemporary marketing are to be unraveled, and if the woes of marketing are to be resolved, there must be some fundamental changes in how corporations think about marketing and some fundamental changes in how marketers market.

MARKETING IS MORE THAN THE SUM OF ITS PARTS

In the first place, marketers must stop thinking about marketing as a series of separate issues or problems. Marketing is a totality of interrelated activities—a change in any component of a marketing program or initiative causes changes in every other component. The issue is *not* to determine how each of the individual marketing activities can be best pursued to cause sales. The issue is how to develop an integrated course of marketing action to create decisive consumer value. To create decisive consumer value, it is necessary to get all the marketing parts to work together in synergy with one another.

This basic idea has a lot of ramifications, as we shall see. For the moment, we concentrate only on its most obvious implication: marketing thinking and marketing programs must be conceived of as integrated entities. For example, a marketing program is *not* integrated if it includes a range of brand variants and advertising to make the individual brand variants seem distinctive while promoting the brand variants to consumers in a way that suggests that each brand variant is no better than the lowest price at which it can be purchased.

Marketing is more than a loose collection of programs or activities that must be individually optimized to cause sales.

This means that the solution of the problems of contemporary marketing are *not* to be found in focusing upon individual marketing activities taken one at a time.

- The problems of contemporary marketing will *not* be resolved through better trade relations, although enhanced trade relations may increase sales, at least in the short term.

- The problems of contemporary marketing will *not* be resolved through the mindless proliferation of brands and brand variants, although a lengthened and/or segmented line of brand offerings may increase sales, at least in the short term.

- The problems of contemporary marketing will *not* be resolved by a continuous spate of consumer price promotions, although such promotions are almost certain to increase sales, at least in the short term.

- The problems of contemporary marketing will *not* be resolved by better advertising campaigns if advertising is debased by brand proliferation and price promotion, although it is always possible that a single, inspired advertising idea may increase sales, at least in the short term.

- The problems of contemporary marketing will *not* be resolved by expanding distribution into new kinds of retail outlets or totally new channels of distribution, although such expansion is likely to increase sales, at least in the short term.

- The problems of contemporary marketing will *not* be resolved by the cost-cutting degradation of brand formulae or brand specifications, although these may maintain sales and increase profits, at least in the short term.

- The problems of contemporary marketing will *not* be resolved by hiring more and more high I.Q., MBA-bearing brand managers, although they can almost certainly be taught to manipulate brand growth to guarantee sales and profit increases, at least in the short term.

The problems of contemporary marketing are a systemic disease: they come about because of the cumulative effect of fragmented, current marketing practices. Marketing's woes cannot be resolved by simply isolating individual marketing practices and reforming them.

It is also true that the systemic failures of marketing vary from corporation to corporation. Not every corporation suffers from systemic marketing failure to the same degree. The more that the corporation defines its long-range objective to be the creation of decisive consumer value, and the less a corporation defines its long-range objective in terms of quarter-to-quarter sales increases, the less likely is systemic marketing disease to be an issue in the corporation.

But the fact that some corporations are less systemically threatened than others should not automatically provide a source of satisfaction to the marketer or the chief executive officer.

Even if the marketer learns to think systemically about marketing problems and issues, there is no guarantee that the problems of contemporary marketing will be resolved. But if the marketer does not learn to think systemically about the marketing issues and problems that have to be faced, it is virtually certain that the problems of contemporary marketing in the company will not soon be resolved.

INTERNAL AND EXTERNAL CHALLENGES

Another way to characterize the woes of contemporary marketing is that they consist of both internal corporate-marketing problems (ill-conceived brand-development guidelines; diffused research and development; brand managers that are trained and rewarded to subordinate all else to quarterly profits) as well as marketing problems that are external to the corporation (the increasing power of the trade; the long-term decline in advertising creativity, and the lack of brand-loyalty proneness among consumers).

It is unlikely that *any* corporation will resolve the problems of contemporary marketing by attempting to solve only the problems that are external to the corporation, meanwhile ignoring those that are internal. In fact, it is almost certainly true that the resolution of trade greed, advertising sameness, and consumer indifference can only be finally settled by addressing and solving *all* internal corporate-marketing problems.

If the final resolution of the contemporary marketing woes depends upon the creation of decisive consumer value, then genuine marketing reform will be accomplished only through two things. There must be a new corporate definition of marketing and a new corporate understanding of just how marketing must work to ensure the future flow of corporate profits.

In the end, the reorientation of the corporation through the redefinition of what marketing is; the redefinition of what the corporation does; and the redefinition of how the corporation will accomplish the basic goal of long-term profitability will force corporations to reconsider the fundamental meaning of competition itself.

We pay a lot of lip service to the competitive ethic, but it is perhaps an appropriate time to think about exactly what competitive mode we really do aspire to. Is it the mode of price competition in which all products are essentially interchangeable and relative consumer value is determined only by the price charged? Or is it the mode of non-price competition in which competitive excellence is determined by the differences that corporations and their marketers are able to build into the products that they offer to their customers? We preach non-price competition in marketing, but we practice, too much, its opposite.

These are hardly new or revolutionary ideas. The Harvard economist Joseph A. Schumpeter expressed similar thoughts as long ago as 1947:

> As soon as quality competition and sales effort are admitted into the sacred precincts of [economic] theory, the price variable is ousted from its dominant position. ... [I]n capitalist reality as distinguished from its textbook picture, it is not that kind of competition which counts but the competition from the new commodity, the new technology, the new source of supply, the new type of organization—competition which commands a decisive cost or quality advantage and which strikes not at the margins of the profits and the outputs of the existing firms but at their foundations and their very lives.[1]

But if a corporation is to dedicate itself to the creation of new consumer value, it must give some thought to redefining its relations with the consumers who are or who will become its customers. In addition, it must define new strategies for delivering products with decisive value to these customers.

It is to these topics that we now turn.

---

[1] Schumpeter, Joseph A., *Capitalism, Socialism, and Democracy*, 2nd Edition, Harper and Brothers Publishers, New York, 1947, p. 84.

Chapter 10

Competition Creates New Value for Consumers

Competition creates the context within which marketing performs. There are a continuum of marketing initiatives that can be planned to deal with competitors. At one extreme, a firm may attempt to achieve competitive equality by matching the moves of its competitors at the tactical level on a move-for-move basis. Such response is almost inevitably reactive—one competitive marketer introduces a lilac-scented version of its best-selling after-shave lotion, and all of its major competitors, shortly thereafter, introduce their own lilac scent in their after-shave lines.

At the other extreme, some firms try, at least some of the time, to win consumer allegiance by continually developing marketing initiatives that are in some way different from those of competitors and, so the marketer hopes, perceived as valuable by consumers. No matter what marketing package of consumer benefits such marketers create, the intent is always to outperform the competition by creating new and decisive consumer value.

There is certainly abundant evidence in the first part of this book that the level of contemporary competitive interaction is often of the first, or reactive, type in many consumer-goods markets, package and durable. It is undoubtedly true that, in addition to all the factors analyzed in Part I that cause the dilemma of marketing, the consumer-goods markets themselves have been so thoroughly explored and exploited over the years that trivial, reactive competitive initiatives are all that many marketers can contemplate. Thus, it might be argued that triviality of initiative is the competitive order of the day and that there is not much that corporations and their marketers can do, beyond matching trivial competitive thrusts with trivial reactive responses.

But it can also be argued that too many marketers are too comfortable and complacent with the game of trivial competitive thrust and parry. These corporations have settled into a frame of mind that does not seek competitive dominance. Corporate America is risk averse. Corporate America finds greatest comfort when it competes in markets that are in equilibrium. As Frederick W. Gluck observes:

> Since most large organizations view change not as an opportunity but as a problem, it is not surprising that they back off from [explosive] change except as a last resort.[1]

But there is probably more to organizational inertia than an inherent resistance to change. Organizations are likely to settle for competition at the level of triviality because that is where marketers themselves are most comfortable. It is easier to respond to competitors in ways that are unlikely to upset sales and profits than to redefine businesses in consumer-value terms to gain competitive advantage. As Kenichi Ohmae puts it:

> But in my experience, managers too often and too willingly launch themselves into old-fashioned competitive battles. It's familiar ground. They know what to do, how to fight. They have a much harder time seeing when an effective customer-oriented strategy could avoid the battle altogether.[2]

It is certainly true that if competition and competitive positions in the market tend to define the overt area of a firm's marketing operations, competition must be attended to. But merely reacting to the competition—no matter how much fun it can be and no matter how it justifies the marketer's role in the corporation—is at best a matter of tactics. The pursuit of competitive dominance through the creation of decisive new consumer value is strategic. Long-term corporate competitiveness must be based on a fundamental understanding of the consumer and an unrelenting determination to consistently serve the consumer better than the consumer will be served by the competition.

Again, as Ohmae observes:

> [Competitive response] cannot come first. First comes painstaking attention to the needs of customers. First comes close analysis of the company's real degrees of freedom in responding to those needs. First comes the willingness to rethink, fundamentally, what products are and what they do, as well as how best to organize the business system that designs, builds, and markets them.[3]

If attention to the needs of consumers is so crucial to the development of competitive dominance and long-term corporate success, it is important to consider how and with what success marketers inform themselves about how consumers perceive value and how marketers deal with consumers' perceptions of value to gain competitive dominance.

HOW WILL THE CORPORATION SERVE THE CONSUMER?

How a company determines its competitive destiny depends a lot on the company, its history, and the ways in which its current management directs its affairs on a day-to-day basis.

Most companies pay a lot of lip service to the "marketing concept," which has a long and glorious tradition in the marketing literature and in the curricula of marketing as it is taught in our leading business schools. Simply defined, the marketing concept is what companies do to make sure their customers are satisfied. The goal of marketing is to create customer satisfaction.

The marking concept may be contrasted with what might be called the "manufacturing concept." Companies that are dominated by the manufacturing concept tend to make what they can make best, regardless of what the consumer wishes and desires.

The marketing concept has been publicly accepted with much enthusiasm by corporations. The idea that the customer *must* be served, no matter what, has characterized the way in which corporations have perceived what it is they do.

But no matter what companies say they do or what companies think they do, the reality of what a company does is determined by actual management decisions as they are made. In the process of real-time decision making the marketing concept may well receive little more than lip service.

It is, however, almost certainly true that almost every successful company has become successful in the first place because it has found a way to attract customers through satisfaction gained from superior products and/or superior services. There are several ways this has been done:

- Sometimes the company has discovered a technology that cannot help but attract consumers when it is made easily accessible at a reasonable price.

- Sometimes a company has unique access to natural resources that are bound to attract consumers when they are properly refined or processed and made accessible at a reasonable price.

- Sometimes the company thinks of a way or develops a strategy to distribute products or services that is more convenient to consumer needs than the distribution practices of competitive companies.

- Sometimes a company finds a way to build a level of quality into its products that has not previously been available at competitive market prices.

- Sometimes a company simply happens to be lucky enough to be in the right place at the right time, gaining initial consumer acceptance with a modest technological or distribution or quality improvement, less because of its inherent excellence than simple good fortune.

Whatever the reason, however, the company does gain initial success. Following this initial success, it must then make a series of strategic decisions that will shape its future and determine whether the company will continue to grow and prosper, or stumble along without much growth, or wither and die.

The point is, of course, that how successful a company ultimately becomes is almost always a result of conscious and, more or less, inspired decisions about how it will serve consumers through the creation of products and services that have identifiable values for consumers.

Alfred P. Sloan, in describing the evolution of the General Motors policy to develop a line of automobiles "for every purse and purpose," catches the essence of this crucial, corporate decision-making process:

Some kind of rational policy was called for. That is, it was necessary to know what one was *trying* to do, apart from the question of what might be imposed upon one by the consumer, the competition, and a combination of technological and economic conditions in the course of evolution.[4]

He continues:

To raise the utility and lower the cost of our cars, one of our first conclusions was that the number of models and the duplication that then existed within the corporation should be limited. By such economizing, which has taken various forms through the years, the corporation, I believe, has rendered the service to the public that all must give in the long run to succeed in business.[5]

Mr. Sloan wrote these words in 1964. Whether he would reach the same conclusions about the service that General Motors and competitive automobile manufacturers have rendered to the public in recent years in disciplining the development of their product lines is, of course, questionable. But his emphasis upon the conscious determination of fundamental corporate policy, "apart from the question of what might be imposed upon one by the consumer, the competition, and a combination of technological and economic conditions," is as pertinent today as ever.

In any event, as the company grows and especially as its interests broaden, the ability to define what it is and to identify the specific marketing space that it will compete within begins to diminish. The meaning of the company and the specific kinds of product or service value that it intends to design and deliver to consumers begins to lose focus and become ill-defined. The vision of the company's founders may be no less clear, but, necessarily, these individuals have a lot of other matters on their minds. As the work force grows, it is increasingly difficult to communicate to its members just what the company is and what it intends to do explicitly for the consumer.

As much as anything else, the ability of the company to maintain the clarity of its direction and the clarity of its intention to deliver value to the consumer determines the degree to which its success will continue.

Meanwhile, however, as the company proceeds along its original path, and sales and profits grow, their maintenance becomes an end in itself. In many firms a fundamental conflict develops between continuing to devote resources to the development of valuable new consumer products/ brands/brand variants and the use of available funds to build and sustain the existing business. Tension grows over choices between the expenditure of earnings to develop and expand existing resources and the diversion of funds into the kinds of activities—research and development, soundly conceived, and proactive marketing research—that may lead to totally new sources of consumer value within the original conception of the firm.

As Danny Miller puts it:

> Increasingly, the central impetus to action becomes the preference of managers, rather than the needs of consumers.[6]

The firm is increasingly bemused by the distinction between competence and will. What the company is currently competent to do is often accepted as the final objective of the firm and the only dependable plan for its future growth. And yet, it is undoubtedly true that the real growth in any business depends as much or more upon its *will* to achieve decisive consumer value rather than merely continuing to pursue, with occasional modifications, what it perceives to be the limit of its current competence.

As this process unfolds, the original impetus to the success of the firm gradually disappears. What is lost is the original ability of the founder or the the dominant manager in the firm to generate new insights into what will appeal to the consumer. What is also lost is the will of the founder or dominant manager that is imposed upon the company to force the acceptance of these genuine insights about how the firm can continue to create customer satisfaction.

And yet, throughout the history of business, it has been the insight, the vision, the belief, and, in the final analysis, the *will* of the gifted innovator— founder, manager, or marketer—that has powered the growth of businesses and companies.

The nature of such insights or visions or beliefs comes about, as often as not, from the immersion of the manufacturer's or marketer's attention upon the product or products that the firm has focused upon; the competitive environment within which they compete; and the constant preoccupation—one should probably say obsession—with the consumer of the product or services of that product/service category.

Not many successor managers or marketers seem to be able to achieve or maintain such intensity of focus upon the consumer/corporate competence/competitive nexus to drive continuously the creation of decisive consumer value. But when one of these unusual people comes along, consumer satisfaction is almost certain to be generated—be it in the form of hula hoops or affordable, dependable automobiles or home-delivered pizza, or fluoridated toothpastes or digitally-recorded compact discs.

Alfred Sloan captured the essence of such insight in the early days of the automobile industry:

> Mr. Ford's assembly-line automobile products, high minimum wages, and low-priced cars were revolutionary and stand among the greatest contributions to our industrial culture. His basic conception of one car in one utility model at an ever-lower price was what the market, especially the farm market, needed at the time. Yet Mr. Durant's feeling for variety in automobiles, however undefined it was then, came closer to the trend of the industry as it evolved in later years.[7]

This quotation raises two issues that are important in thinking about how inspired insights into consumer needs and consumer perceptions of value come about. First, there is nothing, either in the quotation or in the literature, to suggest that either Messrs. Ford or Durant perceived himself to be a marketer, let alone a gifted marketer. The marketing consequences of such insights may well have been enormous, but this has nothing to do with the original insight of the innovator. This suggests that contemporary marketers would do well to keep an open mind about ideas that may have significant marketing potential, no matter who brings such ideas forward in the first place. The creation of customer satisfaction is the responsibility of the entire management of the firm, not merely of the senior marketing executives.

The second implication of the quotation is that fundamental insights about consumers do, indeed, become obsolete, not necessarily as a matter of technology, but as a matter of continuing consumer adaptation to the marketing environment within which they exist. The firm must maintain a continuing understanding of the market as it exists as well as develop insights into how it will evolve in the future if the firm is to survive and prosper.

Thus, the firm must be completely contemporaneous in seeking and defining consumer perceptions of positive value. But this is not enough. Somehow, no matter how large, complex, and multifaceted the firm becomes, it must also *institutionalize* a means for keeping ahead of its competitors in creating decisive value for consumers.

One need only think of how Toyota has defined and redefined consumer value for automobiles in the past 30 years to understand the essence of its competitive success and the essence of the failure of at least some American automobile producers. The ultimate competitive responsibility of the firm is to find ways within itself, within its defined area of competence, within its understanding of how consumers perceive value, and within its understanding of its competitive environment, so that it may consistently excel.

As Franklin S. Houston remarks:

> The marketing concept focuses the marketer's attention on the customer but does not tell the marketer to disregard his or her unique capabilities and resources when deciding how to serve the customer's needs and wants best.[8]

In the final analysis, it is the management of the company and particularly the company's marketers that must assume the responsibility of finding ways to satisfy customers.

CORPORATE GROWTH THROUGH MARKETING INITIATIVE

Everyone agrees that the great marketing insights, the fundamental inspirations—technological or otherwise—that create and shape new markets do not grow on trees.

It is all well and good, therefore, to talk about the days of Ford and Durant in the automobile industry; or the dedication of John Smale, later president of P&G, when, as a product manager, he willed the marketing success of Crest toothpaste through the dogged pursuit of American Dental Association endorsement for the fluoride ingredient; or to try to identify the obscure genius who created the hula-hoop.

But the fundamental question is how one creates marketing successes in the absence of an individual or individuals within the firm who possess the ability to create and impose profound innovation upon markets. Somehow the corporation must find ways to institutionalize growth by producing a continuing stream of marketing innovations that create distinctive and positive value for the consumer, rather than a continuous stream of distinctionless brand variants that cannot command any meaningful or continued customer allegiance.

PAYING ATTENTION TO CONSUMERS

In modern marketing, the link between the consumer and the corporation is provided by marketing research. When it emerged in the early 1920s, the promise of marketing research was that it could provide a flow of information about consumers that managers needed to continuously create new products and services of decisive value. This flow of information would provide a way in which the view of the consumer would always be represented in corporate decision-making processes.

Market research would thus substitute for the kinds of profound insight into how consumers might respond to corporate initiatives that had originally been provided by the insight of the founder or the dominant manager.

Many managers and most marketers have come to view marketing research as the *only* way in which it is possible to gain useful insight into the consumer. They use marketing research to understand what consumers perceive or will perceive to be valuable. They believe that consumers know what is valuable to them and can articulate it to a resourceful market researcher. They also believe that consumers know what they will come to perceive as valuable once they have experienced it and that they can also articulate these future perceptions of satisfaction to the resourceful researcher.

Of course, measuring and interpreting consumer perceptions of value is not as easy as many marketers seem to understand it to be.

Consumers' perceptions of value can be either positive, negative, or neutral. Positive value is what consumers accept with appreciation, negative value is what they avoid if possible, and neutral value neither attracts nor repels them—it evokes no meaningful response at all. Manufacturers often design features into their brands that they believe will be perceived by consumers to have positive value when, in fact, consumers perceive these features to have either negative or neutral value. Marketing often finds it extremely difficult to identify the exact kind of value that consumers will perceive a particular innovation or assertion to possess when they come across it in the marketplace.

No matter what difficulties and ambiguities persist about what consumers either do or will perceive as valuable, marketers spend a great deal of time and money trying to make it easy for consumers to tell them what they want and what they either do or will accept as valuable.

Marketer preoccupation with research on consumer wants, needs, desires, attitudes, daydreams, and whatnot has spawned a major industry in market research. Market research activities are estimated to absorb over $2.5 billion in marketers' money each year.

If the best that this expenditure can do is to support the mindless proliferation of undifferentiated and, thus, valueless brands and brand variants and advertising assertions about them, one can only conclude that marketers are not getting their money's worth.

And yet, if marketers do believe that their market research money is well spent, it either means that market research provides a comfortable rationale for marketers as they proliferate brands, or it means that marketers simply still do not have a meaningful conception of the consumer they seek to please, in spite of all this marketing research, or both.

In either case, it seems clear that there is something missing in the relationship between marketers and marketing research. In fact, marketing research, in spite of the marketers' faith in and support of it, appears to be little more than a collaborator in causing the business problems that confront marketing.

THE FAILURE OF MARKETING RESEARCH

How can it be that marketing research has done so little to resolve the dilemma of marketing? It is difficult to generalize about any activity that is as diffuse and idiosyncratic as marketing research. But two general flaws are obvious.

What Consumers Know

The first flaw is the erroneous assumption that consumers know and can articulate what they like.

Marketers believe that consumers can tell what they want or what they will respond to. Marketers believe that consumers can predict how they will act in the marketplace at some future time when they are presented with a particular product or advertisement or other marketing stimulus in a particular marketing research project.

It may very well be true that consumers can, at least some of the time, validly predict what they will do when confronted with a product or advertisement that differs significantly from those that they are used to seeing. Too often, however, what consumers are asked to reflect upon represents such a minor variation from what is presently available in the market that their present response to the product or advertisement under study has no meaningful or predictive relation to any future response or action.

For example, much focus-group interviewing, in contemporary practice, suffers from this shortcoming. Some sort of brand or communication variant is presented to a group of consumers, and they are asked to respond to it. Often enough, the variant that is presented to the group represents some trivial reslicing of old advertising or brand development baloney.

The respondents, in the social situation created by the group itself, believe that they are expected to take all this seriously. Instead of appearing stupid before their peers and their interrogators, the respondents will respond at will, arguing with and challenging each other, randomly articulating whatever seemingly reasonable and socially acceptable thoughts come to mind. If the research topic is real enough to be the subject of a group session, then, surely, reason the captive respondents, it must be meaningful enough to justify responsive group conversation and reaction, no matter how mindless or invalid it may, in fact, be.

Meanwhile, the marketers themselves listen with rapt attention, grasping at each consumer insight and provocative statement, seeking always a justification for their next marketing action in the words of the beguiled respondents. It is an article of faith with too many marketers that consumer statements in such sessions reveal marketing truth. One wonders how many marketing pipedreams and wasted marketing resources are generated each year on the basis of such endorsements as, "It was gangbusters in the focused group sessions."

What Research Measures

The second general flaw in marketing research is that research measurements do not measure consumer reality.

Even more insidious is the notion that many research measurements measure something that is truly relevant to marketing decisions, rather than what the researchers who have created the measurement think is relevant.

A case in point is the evaluation of consumer response to advertising (copy research) as it has been practiced in marketing for at least the last 40 years.

Some researchers agree that what consumers recall from an advertising message, some time after they have been exposed to that message, is a valid measure of the effect of that creative advertising idea. Of course, this is only true if the advertising content is meaningful and important to consumers to begin with.

There is no evidence anywhere that high recall of an irrelevant or ineffective message demonstrates advertising effectiveness. In fact, some advertising features executional elements—curvaceous women, dogs, cats, small children, whatever—that often deliver high recall of advertising content no matter what the advertisement itself says about the product. Nevertheless, if a recall measure of advertising content is made, it is often assumed by marketers that since the measurement exists and purports to measure advertising effectiveness, that it does, in fact, measure advertising effectiveness.

But even the research community is far from unanimous in its endorsement of content recall as a measurement of advertising effect. Other researchers believe that advertising effectiveness can be measured by changes in stated brand preference measured before and after exposure to an advertisement. Again, there is little serious evidence that changes in stated brand preference, before and after exposure to a commercial, consistently demonstrates advertising effectiveness, except the evidence that at least some research practitioners accept such measures as valid.

It should come as little surprise that when the same advertisements are tested *both* for content recall and, separately, for their ability to stimulate changes in stated brand preference, the results are often contradictory. When one measures different aspects of a stimulus, it often turns out that the results are different, even though the stimulus itself is unchanged from measurement to measurement. To overcome this problem, some researchers now advocate the combination of measures of content recall and brand-preference stimulation in the same research procedure, thus giving the marketer the best of two worlds and seriously reducing the likelihood that any single advertisement will pass muster on both measures of purported effectiveness.

There is no evidence of any kind that either or both of these measures of advertising effect has improved the performance of advertising during the period of over 40 years in which these measures have been in vogue, let alone done anything at all to forestall the long-term decline in advertising creativity that we observed in Chapter 6.

Probably, as Alfred Politz—who was a leading market researcher in his lifetime and a profound one at that—has implied, both of these methods (and the combination of the two) measure, too much, the artifice of advertising and measure, too little, its substance:

> It is ... the function of perfect advertising to step behind its own means— its own tricks and gimmicks—and push the product so much into the foreground that the advertising itself, psychologically speaking, can be overlooked.[9]

The point is not that all copy testing is irrelevant or that any copy testing at all is worthless, for this is almost certainly not the case. The point is that the making of a measurement does not guarantee its relevance. The marketer too often accepts the measurement for what it purports to be, rather than accepting it only if it truly conforms to a vision—if the marketer has such a vision—of what consumers will come to value in products, advertisements, or other marketing entities.

Another example of the blind acceptance of research measurements has to do with market segmentation. Much of the marketing research work that underlies the identification of market segments is based upon a statistical technique called factor analysis. The technique is structured so that consumers are asked to evaluate products or brands on the basis of long lists of attributes. Some consumers choose some attributes to describe or evaluate a product or brand in a category while other consumers choose other attributes to describe the products or brands.

Consumers may thus be grouped or segmented on the basis of the groups of attributes that they tend to choose. The resulting groups of consumers are then taken to imply that products or brands with some differ-ence—usually marginal—will appeal to these different groups or segments. Thus, the research finding validates the idea that marketing segments exist and provides a rationalization for segmented marketing based on small—possibly even meaningless—differences in consumer perceptions of products or brands.

The problem with all of this is that if one starts with a statistical pro-cedure that produces segments, one ends up with segments and, thus, with implied products to satisfy these segments and their imputed preference differences.

Once again, there is no serious evidence that this popular approach consistently or even occasionally produces definitions of product oppor-tunity that have any positive or distinctive value to real consumers in real markets on real shopping expeditions.

In fact, Andrew Ehrenberg's toothpaste data (see Chapter 7) suggest that there is little, if any, more inclination for customers to be loyal to segmented products than to the normal run of products. And yet, why seg-ment brands unless such segmentation provides a basis for brand loyalty?

Stephen Jay Gould makes the general case against factor analysis (in this instance, in connection with the identification of human attributes such as intelligence):

> My complaint lies with the practice of assuming that the mere existence of a factor, in itself, provides a license for causal speculation. Factorists have consistently warned against such an assumption, but our Platonic urges to discover underlying essences continue to prevail over proper caution.[10]

The issue is not with the practice of market research as such. The problem lies rather with the marketers' tendency to accept any research re-sult at all, simply because it is research and simply because the researcher tells the marketer that the finding has relevance to the making of a particular marketing decision. Too often the researcher has simply measured what was measurable without any thought at all about the meaning or relevance of the resulting measurement to marketing or, for that matter, to anything else.

What is missing in all of this is that neither the marker researcher nor the marketer can or will assume responsibility for the validity of the measures made by marketing research. If the marketing researcher does not participate in any meaningful way in final marketing decisions, that researcher has little concern or interest in how the marketing research findings end up being used. If, on the other hand, the marketer blithely assumes that a research measurement is what it purports to be, there can be no control exerted by the marketer over the effect that research findings have on decisions. What gets lost in this shuffle of missing responsibility is the promise of market research.

Either researchers must participate in the marketing decisions that their work influences, or marketers must insist that research measurements, whatever they may be, are compatible with the marketers' visions of what is valuable to consumers either in advertisements, in brands, or in brand variants. As long as researchers accept no responsibility for the decision and marketers accept no responsibility for the measurement, the contribution that marketing research can make to marketing is either limited or detrimental or both.

There is little question that the dependence of marketers upon marketing research has not done much to inform the marketer in any profoundly practical way about consumer perceptions of value. Marketers and market researchers must somehow, sometime, somewhere reach an agreement about what marketing is really all about. Too much research attention is focused upon consumer speculations and predictions about what will be valuable to them in the future. Too much research attention is focused upon measurements that have not been explicitly developed to identify consumer perceptions of value.

This lack of agreement about what marketing is and how marketing must serve the consumer has two implications as we pursue the goal of trying to define what consumers will perceive to be valuable:

- First of all, the creation of consumer value cannot stem from an unquestioning dependence upon marketing research as it has been practiced in the past. Part of the problem is that marketers have paid too little attention to how consumers really act and think. They have, instead, left it to the researchers. Researchers tend to be more interested in what they can measure easily than in its relation to the reality of marketing. It is easy, for example, to measure commercial recall or brand preference changes and to define market segments on the basis of factor analysis. Researchers promote what is easily measured, because they have no direct responsibility in the application of their measures in the practice of marketing.

- Secondly, the only way in which researchers can be made responsible for their measurements is to involve the researchers in their use. The separation of marketing research from marketing practice—no matter

what the reasons—has done more to force researchers to preoccupy themselves with what is easily measurable than any other phenomenon in contemporary marketing. Marketers may or may not be smart to begin with, but
they are sure to end up dumb if they do not question the explicit relevance
of research measures to the specific decisions that they must make.

Nobel laureates in science do not let others do their critical
experiments for them.

This basic issue between marketers and marketing researchers is well
summarized by Fred Huser:

> We do a lot of testing. I think the key is in market testing rather than
> [market research department] testing, because so often I think it is diffi-
> cult for the MRD people to convincingly tell you that there is a strong
> correlation between the results that they are showing you and what is go-
> ing to happen in the marketplace.[11]

The trouble is that marketing research measures do not predict what
will subsequently happen in the marketplace. They cannot assess what is
valuable to consumers nor what will become valuable to them in the future.

WHAT'S A MARKETER TO DO?

Marketing in many corporations finds it difficult to create new kinds of consumer satisfaction. It is frustrated because the management of the corporation and its day-to-day decision making have lost the flair for understanding
what will give the consumer the satisfaction that led to the corporation's success in the first place.

A tension exists within the marketing function because of the need to
maximize sales and profits from the existing products of the corporation and
the conflicting need to create new brands and brand variants that will create
decisive, new consumer value.

The marketing function, meanwhile, does not get much help from the
market researchers in the creation of such new consumer value because they
have little interest in and less responsibility for the corporation's ultimate
marketing decisions and the grounds upon which they are made.

It is the marketer's function to formulate strategies that will help the
corporation to prosper and grow. One such strategy is to proliferate

distinctionless brands and brand variants. It is the logical consequence of all of the internal marketing frustrations that we have just listed.

In addition, marketers often formulate strategies to increase corporate sales or profits that look outside the corporation for their inspiration. Such strategies generally signal at least a partial abdication of marketing and the marketing function from the creative internal-development process—such as it is—that is supposed to create new satisfaction for consumers.

These externally focused strategies are:

■ The strategy of trade accommodation

■ The extension of marketing power through mergers, takeovers, and acquisitions

■ The elimination of marginal brand, brand variants, or businesses to increase profitability

The basic question is whether or not these externally focused growth strategies provide the institutional means to create decisive, new consumer value and resolve the dilemma of marketing.

The next chapter will evaluate each of these externally focused growth strategies in terms of the marketing issues that, in the final analysis, determine long-term corporate growth:

1. Does the strategy encourage the search for decisive consumer value and genuine competitive excellence? Does it diminish the corporate tendency to proliferate distinctionless brands and brand variants?

2. Does the strategy permit the corporation to change itself organizationally to pursue competitive excellence?

3. Does the strategy encourage the development and acceptance of innovative ideas from any source within the corporation? Does it reward such innovative ideas when they prove out?

---

[1] Gluck, Frederick W., "'Big Bang' Management," *The Journal of Business Strategy,* Summer, 1985, p. 60.

[2] Reprinted by permission of Harvard Business Review. "Getting Back to Strategy," by Kenichi Ohmae (November/December 1988), p. 150. Copyright © 1988 by the President and Fellows of Harvard College, all rights reserved.

[3] Ibid., p. 149.

[4] Sloan, Alfred P., Jr., *My Years With General Motors*, Doubleday & Company, New York, 1964, p. 60.

[5] Ibid., p. 64.

[6] The ICARUS PARADOX, copyright © 1990 by Danny Miller. Reprinted by permission of HarperBusiness, a division of HarperCollins Publishers, Inc.

[7] Sloan, Alfred P., Jr., *My Years With General Motors*, Doubleday & Company, Inc., New York, 1964, p. 4.

[8] Houston, Franklin S., "The Marketing Concept: What It Is and What It Is Not," *The Journal of Marketing*, April, 1986, p. 86.

[9] Politz, Alfred, "The Dilemma of Creative Advertising," *Journal of Marketing* 25:2, October, 1960, p. 5.

[10] Gould, Stephen Jay, *The Mismeasure of Man*, W.W. Norton & Company, New York, 1981, p. 268.

[11] Huser, Fred, "How Do You Maximize Creativity In Your Advertising... In Your Sales Promotion... In Both?" *Advertising Management Conference Showcase*, Association of National Advertisers, Inc., New York, 1990, p. 39.

Chapter 11

Internal Strategies for Corporate Growth

Corporations can usually describe quite confidently the strategies that they will pursue to increase future sales and profits. These strategies of growth are usually articulated specifically in terms of the ways in which the corporation currently runs its business. They enunciate the steps that will be taken by the corporation to achieve specific sales and profits goals.

What these strategies for growth almost never do is to articulate how the corporation itself must change to achieve any increase in sales and profits at all or to accelerate their growth. These strategies inevitably assume that the current corporate ways of doing business provide an adequate framework for future corporate growth. Thus, these strategies generally provide for an extension of existing corporate activities or for a modification of these activities within existing corporate research and development, financial, manufacturing, and sales and marketing initiatives and programs. The key question about all of this is, of course, whether the existing corporate structure is capable of creating decisive, new consumer value.

In this chapter, we will begin an evaluation of several strategies for corporate growth to determine whether they are well suited, or suited at all, to creating new, decisive consumer value.

THE STRATEGY OF BRAND AND BRAND-VARIANT PROLIFERATION

The most pervasive strategy for increasing corporate sales and profits is the strategy of brand and brand-variant proliferation. It is the strategy that we have examined in some detail in the preceding pages. Its conspicuous flaw is that it rarely creates new and decisive value for the consumer. Neither does the strategy of brand and brand-variant proliferation make advertising more useful or informative; promote brand loyalty; nor reduce increasing sameness among products.

As far as the criteria of Chapter 10 are concerned, this strategy:

- Does not encourage the search for decisive new consumer value

- Does nothing to encourage the corporation to reorganize its product development and marketing activities

- Does nothing to encourage the development of innovative ideas in the service of the ultimate consumer

THE STRATEGY OF TRADE ACCOMMODATION

Another corporate strategy for growth has been to emphasize the improvement of trade relations. If one of the obvious problems with marketing in the early 1990s is the intransigence and greediness of the trade, an obvious solution for marketers is to cozy up to their trade customers.

In the marketing heyday of the 1960s and 1970s, most consumer-goods marketers treated their trade customers with greater or lesser contempt. Marketers created demand for their brands through unique product designs and through advertising pressure. The retailer was forced to accede to this created demand by stocking shelves with the products that their customers —the ultimate consumer—desired. In this scenario the retailer was odd person out because marketers were able directly to influence the ultimate consumer.

The revolution in retailing that we have recounted in Chapter 4 was bound, sooner or later, to force marketers to deal in a different way with the retail trade. Retailers have become an independent marketing force—they can decide whether to stock or not stock a marketer's brands and at what price to offer them on their shelves. And the retailer can directly influence the ultimate consumer through the retailer's own price promotion. Meanwhile, the marketer's brands have lost the distinctiveness that they once had, and the power of brand advertising to create direct consumer pressure on retailer stocking practices has seriously declined.

These increases in the power of retailers have forced the marketer not only to accommodate the retailer in a general way but also to customize this retailer accommodation in ways that are appropriate to specific, competitive retail situations in specific geographic areas. All of a sudden we have begun to hear marketers proclaiming that all markets are "local" and that all markets are "retail." Such proclamations merely reflect the marketers' growing realization that if dominant retailers are not accommodated on an individual basis, sales and profits will be lost no matter what other marketing forces are deployed by the marketer.

Marketers are thus faced with the dual problem of making retailers happier and more responsive to the marketer's wishes, while, if possible, reducing or making more efficient the escalating direct promotional cost of doing any business with the retailer at all.

An early manifestation of this new attitude surfaced in the 1980s, when companies like Kraft General Foods, Frito–Lay, Quaker Oats, P&G, General Mills, and Nabisco, among others, began to talk about developing "partnership" relations with leading retailers. When one party to a marketing transaction starts using the word *partnership* in describing its relation with another party to the transaction, it means that the first party has become subservient to the other. The difficulty in "partnerships" is, of course, that the dominant partner gains considerably less from a close and interactive relationship with the subservient partner than does the subservient partner.

In reality, trade "partnerships" mean that corporate marketers are willing to revise their own marketing and distribution practices, unilaterally, to accommodate important retailers. As marketers hasten to make such accommodations, there is, of course, the hope that they will make important retailers better customers by developing business processes and practices that the retailer will like. Secondarily, there is also the possibility that such new processes and practices will reduce the marketer's own distribution costs and, thus, increase its profits. Both objectives have been assiduously pursued by leading marketing companies.

The way this might work, as the *New York Times* observed, was that the existence of the "partnership" would:

> ... cut inventories for both parties, smooth out production schedules and quickly identify service and quality problems. They are looking for the same kind of benefits that automakers and other industrial companies have been reaping in recent years from "just-in-time" delivery arrangements with suppliers.[1]

Not only have the new "partnerships" worked toward streamlining supply and inventory relations between marketers and retailers, they have also led to a growing professionalism in the sales service provided by marketers to dominant retailers. Most retailers would prefer to deal with one senior representative of a multiple brand or division company, for example, than with individual salespersons representing each brand or division.

This has led to the creation of a single sales contact point between many marketers and their major retail customers. And that single-sales contact usually has sufficient authority to modify its company's practices immediately in ways that will ingratiate the customer to the company. Thus, as *Business Week* reports, P&G has worked toward the resolution of several major irritations at Wal-Mart through its senior contact with that important customer:

> In the past year, P&G has moved a dozen officials to Arkansas to develop a joint strategy with the big, Bentonville-based retailer. Can both companies use the same number to identify an item, eliminating a need to reticket each shipping container when it arrives? Can P&G adapt its up-and-down pricing to Wal-Mart's everyday-low-price approach?[2]

There is no question that the corporate strategy of accommodating the retail trade in whatever ways possible will strengthen trade relations. How could such a corporate strategy not accomplish this important, if limited, end? And such strengthening may even lead to increased sales, lower costs, and increased profits for the marketer.

But does this heightened coziness with the trade lead the marketer to do anything to benefit the ultimate consumer?

Does it provide the ultimate consumer with better products?

Does it reduce brand proliferation and product sameness?

Does it make advertising more informative and more useful to the consumer?

Does it motivate consumers to become more brand loyal, either consciously or unconsciously?

Does trade accommodation, in summary, create decisive new consumer value? The clear answer is that there is nothing in the accommodation of trade customers that helps the marketer better serve the ultimate consumer of its products.

Only when the marketer's competitive impotence is defined in retail-trade terms does this marketing strategy for growth aid the marketer. By accommodating the trade, sales may be increased and marketing costs may be reduced. Thus, profits may be increased. But these are, at best, tactical competitive gains within the channels of distribution. Like all tactical competitive gains, they are likely to be short-lived because they are, at least in principle, equally available to competitive companies with the will to achieve them.

The sales that are gained and the profits that are made by trade ingratiation are, after all, sales and profits only from existing product lines and proliferated brands and brand variants. If anything, the coddling of the trade merely reinforces existing practices in product definition and development, it does not reform them.

Thus, in applying the criteria of Chapter 10 to the marketing strategy for sales and profit growth through trade accommodation, we conclude that:

- This strategy does not encourage the search for decisive, new consumer value.

- This strategy does nothing to encourage the corporation to reorganize its development and marketing of brands.

- This strategy does nothing to encourage the development of innovative ideas in the service of the ultimate consumer.

THE STRATEGY OF INCREASING CORPORATE SIZE TO INCREASE MARKETING POWER

Another strategy to increase corporate sales and profits is to increase the scope of corporate operations. The idea is to accumulate brands and brand variants through corporate mergers and acquisitions and, among other things, increase the critical mass, power, and efficiency of marketing in the process.

Thus, for example, it was the inherent value of brands and the potential marketing power that they represented that drove the bidding for Nabisco in 1988. As the *New York Times* reported after an offer of $26.8 billion had been made for the company:

The huge price is a measure of the value that big corporations now place on acquiring proven business lines rather than developing and building products on their own. ...

No company would make a $20 billion commitment to developing new products, but nearly that much will probably be paid in total as companies fight over the pieces of RJR Nabisco as it is carved up and sold off.[3]

Clearly, if no company would make a $20 billion commitment to develop new products, the acquisition of existing and successful brands offers an alternative route to the growth of sales as well as to the growth of marketing activities and budgets.

There are at least three elements entwined in these corporate mergers and acquisitions. One has to do with the financial implications of such activities, but the other two deal with the enhancement of marketing power.

In the first place, there are always financial implications in corporate acquisitions and mergers. The explicit purpose of the "deal" is to realize the true value of the assets of the company that is to be acquired or merged. In the process of acquisition or merger, the engineers of the deal, as is taken for granted, will not harm themselves financially.

But it is also always assumed, explicitly or implicitly, that there is previously untapped marketing power in the newly combined assets, and it is these unrealized values that provide the rationale for the deal itself. The financial implication of such acquisitions and mergers has nothing at all to do with marketing, except insofar as the financial deal itself assumes some sort of reality as a result of these marketing consequences.

The first marketing implication of such acquisitions or mergers is that marketing skills that already exist in the host company are transferable to the target company. Thus, it is assumed that skillful marketers can always breathe new life and growth into existing brands that the target company has never been able to force to their true potential. Thus, for example, P&G always seems to assume that its marketing know-how will transform the operations of the companies that it acquires.

Essentially, such transfer of marketing skill means that whatever marketing expertise the host company has will now be infused into the target company. Such infusion of marketing expertise has little to do with the creation of new consumer value, at least in the typical host company, for, as we have seen, the typical company rarely creates absolute consumer value when it markets according to its normal competitive pattern. So, the transfer of imputed marketing skills that are presumed to be superior has little to do with the resolution of contemporary marketing problems. The increase in marketing power, whatever else it may accomplish, holds no benefit, implicit or explicit, for the consumer.

A case in point is the acquisition of Crush International by P&G in the early 1980s. P&G is, arguably, the most knowledgeable and experienced marketing company in the world. When it acquired Crush, it presumably believed that its marketing experience could transform and revolutionize the marketing activities of Crush. In the end, P&G failed to make much of an impact upon the sales and profits of Crush. Perhaps it failed because it overestimated the ultimate consumer appeal of orange- and root beer–flavored soft drinks. Perhaps it failed because it ignored the inherent power and intractability of the local bottler in the successful marketing of soft-drink products. As *Advertising Age* pointed out:

> In its efforts to work with the bottlers, some sources say, P&G was not sensitive to the traditional way of doing business in the soft-drink industry, which still relies heavily on personal contact.[4]

But, perhaps even more important than P&G's positive mistakes in dealing with the soft-drink industry and its idiosyncrasies was its dependence upon basic marketing skills that had almost always been transferable to other product categories. This time, the transfer of skills simply did not seem to take:

> "The [P&G] Crush people probably brought more to the table in marketing research, advertising and merchandising programs than any other product [people] that we do business with," said Mr. Bodnar, [a] bottler. "They are truly marketeers."[5]

The final element in such deals is the implicit notion that there are economies of scale in marketing operations. Not only are marketing skills transferable, but the agglomeration of marketing efforts and resources leads to enhanced efficiency in marketing.

The idea seems to be that the predecessor company has never quite reached the critical marketing mass that guarantees ultimate marketing efficiency. Big marketing means efficient marketing. Part of such scale economies presumably comes from the full utilization of individual marketers' skills and the consequent ability to apply more varied and more directed talent to any specific marketing task that may arise.

In addition, some of the scale economies presumably come from the company's enhanced ability to access and utilize the best talent in the best marketing-service organizations—advertising agencies, sales promotion houses, direct response agencies, public relations firms, and so forth.

And some of the scale economies presumably come from increased bargaining power in the marketplace—the ability, for example, to command superior resources at lower prices. Thus, larger marketers may buy advertising-agency service at more favorable rates than their smaller competitors because they can force the advertising agencies to pass along their own economies of scale that derive from larger advertising accounts. Or larger marketers may be able to negotiate more favorable media prices since they routinely buy more media space or time than do their smaller competitors. Or larger marketers may be able to avail themselves of cross-brand or interactive promotional schemes that the smaller advertiser has neither the resources nor the brand inventory to mount.

Whatever the specific marketing benefit may be, it is usually true that the larger marketers will be able to market more effectively and efficiently, simply because the resources that they now command exceed those of either of the predecessor marketing operations.

But the final effects of such enlarged operations due to acquisitions and mergers are only found—if they be found at all—in lower costs or more efficient operations of the marketer because of the agglomeration of sales. This increased scale creates nothing of value for the consumer. Like enhanced trade relations, this growth strategy does not provide consumers with better products; does not reduce brand proliferation and product sameness; does not make advertising more informative and useful to consumers; nor does it give the consumer any basis for becoming more brand loyal.

Competitive efficiency and effectiveness that results in enhanced corporate profits immediately is, as we have repeatedly seen, inherently different from competitive excellence in the products offered by the marketer to the consumer. Corporate profitability does not create consumer value or competitive excellence in and of itself. In fact, enhanced corporate profits are often achieved only at the expense of competitive excellence and consumer satisfaction.

Applying the evaluative criteria developed in Chapter 10 to the corporate strategy of growth through increasing corporate size, we conclude:

- This strategy does not encourage the search for decisive new consumer value.

- This strategy does not encourage the corporation to reorganize the development and marketing of brands.

- This strategy does nothing to encourage the development of innovative ideas in the service of the ultimate consumer.

THE STRATEGY OF CORPORATE PROFIT GROWTH THROUGH THE ELIMINATION OF BRANDS AND BUSINESSES

A corporate strategy aimed primarily at increasing profits but not sales is the strategy of eliminating unprofitable businesses or brands. Under this strategy, the weak sisters in the corporate array of brands and businesses are identified and eliminated. An attendant feature of this strategy is that corporate resources previously diffused among a greater number of brands and businesses can now be focused on the growth and improvement of the remaining brands and businesses. In a sense, the corporate strategy of brand and business elimination is almost the opposite of corporate growth through acquisition and merger.

This strategy of elimination—of refocusing corporate attention on the core businesses of the corporation—is usually rationalized in one of three ways:

1. The corporation must reduce wanton creativity.

2. The corporation must reduce brand overlap.

3. Future growth is inhibited by the number of existing brands and brand variants.

Wanton Creativity

In some companies the elimination of brands and businesses is justified because management comes to believe that the company's marketers have become overly creative and imaginative in the development of new brands and brand variants without paying proper attention to their profit potential. The attention of the marketers has become focused upon the products that the company is able to make. But no one pays enough attention to whether consumers will buy these products in sufficient quantity. Such overzealous creativity in the development of new brands and especially brand variants certainly contributes to their proliferation.

The Campbell Soup Company has apparently been troubled with this kind of unrestrained creativity in the development and introduction of new brands and brand variants in past years. (See, for example, the Campbell chicken noodle soup variants in Exhibit 2–3.) Thus, in 1990, the company formally adopted the strategy of business elimination to increase corporate profits, under the guidance of its new CEO, David W. Johnson. Johnson's assessment of the Campbell situation was simply that its new product activities—provocative and exciting as they might be on a product-by-product basis—had become totally undisciplined. There was too much new product creativity going on all at once. The result was that Campbell's over-all marketing activity had become unfocused, and the profitability of the corporation had become imperiled. As Mr. Johnson put it in an interview with the *New York Times*:

> When we start putting points on the board–not by winning marketing awards or posting records for new product introduction, but by actual profits—then people are going to love it.[6]

Campbell employees had, even before the advent of Mr. Johnson, sensed a problem. As Campbell's vice president of marketing research, who certainly must have had some role in the development of many unprofitable Campbell brands and brand variants in previous years, put it in 1990:

> We're definitely blowing the whistle on mindless line extensions.[7]

Not only were new product introductions severely curtailed, but existing lines were either shortened or discontinued. In the end there will be fewer brands with the Campbell name on them, and there will be fewer Campbell brand variants within the product lines that are maintained.

Brand Overlap

Some companies have developed several brands within the same product category as has P&G, for example, in the heavy detergent field. (Exhibit 11–1 shows P&G brand entries in the heavy-duty detergent field in 1992.) Sometimes individual brands or brand variants are indistinguishable from competing brands or brand variants produced by the same companies. Such brand duplication and overlap is, of course, at the heart of brand and brand-variant proliferation.

When such brand/brand-variant overlap is rationalized, it is almost inevitable that the number of competing company brands and variants can be reduced so that each brand/brand variant is distinctive in some way, at least insofar as other brands produced by the company are concerned. A case in point is the detergent brands marketed by the Colgate–Palmolive Company:

EXHIBIT 11–1   P&G heavy-duty powdered detergent brand variants—1992

... Colgate decided that the company had more detergent brands than it needed and reduced the number it sold from seven to four. Instead of overlapping, each brand has a distinct market position. ...[8]

This kind of effort assuredly reduces the amount of brand/brand-variant proliferation within the product lines of a company that imposes such discipline upon itself. As such, it has a certain value in reducing the proliferation of brands, but it will not cure brand/brand-variant proliferation among competing product lines unless all manufacturers ultimately reduce overlap in their product lines.

Inhibited Growth

Some companies become concerned about the sheer number of brands and brand variants that they market because this number has grown to a point where future sales and profit growth is, itself, inhibited. In such companies it is the breadth and depth of existing product lines that causes concern because they somehow limit the freedom that the company has in exploiting new opportunities.

The need to cut back on this kind of brand and brand–variant proliferation is an issue, for example, in companies that depend upon a specific, limited physical facility in the distribution of their products. For example, if the company delivers to store door, the number of brands and brand variants that it markets can be limited by the physical size of its standard delivery trucks. Or when a company provides pegboard racks to retailers for the display of its product line, the number of brands and brand variants that it markets is limited by the physical capacity of its racks.

In companies of this kind the entire array of brands and brand variants is sometimes subjected to scrutiny in order to identify those items in the line that are least beneficial to the company.

One major biscuit company—a traditional store-door deliverer—conducted a major test of a dramatically shortened product line in several test markets to determine the effect that the shortened line would have upon sales and profits. The test stores were stocked with about 75 percent of the brands and brand variants from the full product line.

In the test stores, total sales declined by 9 percent—somewhat less than expected since the deleted items accounted for about 13 percent of total company sales. But it was estimated that company profits would improve overall by 14 percent if the shortened line performed as well in a national expansion. In addition, there was virtually no reduction in the shelf space allotted to this marketer in the test stores as a result of the stock deletions brought about by the test. Thus, the remaining items in the line were permitted by the retailers to absorb the shelf space previously used by the deleted brands.

In spite of the undeniable success of this test, there was major resistance within the company to a national rollout of the shortened line of products. Too many of the deleted products had been in the line too long—they were a part of the culture of the company. Veteran employees simply could not conceive of their company marketing a line of products that did not contain the deleted items.

One of the major supports for proliferated brand lines—both for companies with physical constraints in their distribution systems and for companies without such constraints—is the reluctance to remove established brand names or brand variants from the product lines.

As Philip Kotler has pointed out, it is not uncommon for weak brands or brand variants to be retained in a product line for rational, if superficial, reasons: sales are certain to improve in the next quarter; the marketing program, not the product, is deficient; the product will sell more when the design or formulation is modified; its sales volume covers costs and absorbs overhead; etc. Kotler continues:

> But there are also situations where the persistence of weak products can only be explained by the presence of vested interests, management or consumer sentiment, or just plain corporate inertia. A lot of people inside or outside an organization grow to depend upon a particular product.[9]

So even when there is a will to prune out weaker products from a product line that has become proliferated, it is often not easy to do. When it is done successfully, there is evidence that any loss in sales is offset with a gain in profit, and this is certainly enough to recommend it as a viable corporate strategy, at least to achieve profit growth.

Yet when companies do manage to eliminate brands or variants, the question remains whether and to what extent this corporate gain is likely to help consumers. It is certainly true that such line pruning will reduce the number of brands and brand variants that face the consumer in a retail store. There may be some reduction in consumer frustration or confusion or indecision among brands. But, as in the case of other corporate strategies that increase profits and/or increase sales, the benefit tends to accrue almost exclusively to the corporation rather than to the ultimate consumer.

Eliminations of brands and brand variants from a product line is a negative rather than a positive corporate act from the standpoint of the consumer. This is true whether the products are eliminated as a reaction to unrestrained creativity in new product programs; as a result of the rationalization of existing product lines; or as a result of a conscious effort to reduce the total number of brands and brand variants marketed by the company.

The strategy of product elimination does reduce, at least slightly, the proliferation of one marketer's brands and brand variants, and it does reduce, at least slightly, some brand sameness. But there is nothing inherent in this strategy that provides consumers with more valuable products; that makes brand advertising more informative or more useful; or that develops increased consumer brand loyalty.

Thus, in the final analysis the strategy of brand elimination—like the strategies of brand proliferation, trade accommodation, or increasing corporate size to enhance corporate marketing power—may increase corporate sales and profits but does little to resolve the fundamental problems of contemporary marketing. In terms of the Chapter 10 criteria, the strategy of brand or business elimination does not encourage the search for decisive consumer value; does nothing to encourage corporations to reorganize the development or marketing of its brands; and does nothing to encourage the corporate development of innovative ideas in the service of the ultimate consumer.

---

[1] "Moving the Pampers Faster Cuts Everybody's Costs," *New York Times*, July 14, 1991, p. F–5.

[2] "Stalking the New Consumer," *Business Week*, August 28, 1989, p. 62.

[3] "RJR Nabisco Gets $26.8 Billion Plan from First Boston," *New York Times*, November 21, 1988 p. A–1.

[4] "Crush Fails to Fit on P&G Shelf," *Advertising Age*, July 10, 1989, p. 42.

[5] Ibid. p. 43.

[6] "Campbell Cutting 364 from Staff," *New York Times*, May 2, 1990, p. D-1.

[7] "M'm! M'm! Bad! Trouble at Campbell Soup," *Business Week*, September 25, 1989, p. 69.

[8] "The Marketing Revolution at Procter & Gamble," *Business Week*, July 25, 1988, p. 76.

[9] Reprinted by permission of Harvard Business Review. "Phasing Out Weak Products," by Philip Kotler (March/April 1965), p. 110. Copyright © 1965 by the President and Fellows of Harvard College, all rights reserved.

Chapter 12

Value Creation Strategies for Corporate Growth

Preceding chapters discussed four externally-focused strategies that are followed by corporations to increase sales or profits or both: the strategy of brand proliferation; the strategy of trade accommodation; the strategy of increasing corporate size to increase marketing power; and the strategy of brand and business elimination. As we have seen, none of these strategies delivers any significant benefit to the consumer, no matter what their effect upon the sales and profits of the corporation may be.

This chapter considers a more inward looking and much riskier corporate strategy for increasing sales and profits. It is the value creation strategy.

CREATING DECISIVE NEW CONSUMER VALUE

If there is one thing that most corporate leaders say that their corporations do, and even probably believe that their corporations do, it is to create decisive consumer value. One would be hard pressed, indeed, to find a corporate leader who asserted that the enterprise's strategy for long-term growth was merely to adopt one or more of the strategies that were discussed in Chapter 11.

Imagine a captain of industry standing before an annual stockholders' meeting and saying words to the effect that: "Our destiny will be found in the proliferation of copycat brands and brand variants that are undistinguished in any way from those of our competitors." Or, "Our corporate future will be built upon the accommodation and gratification of our very dear friends in the retail trade." Such utterances are unlikely to occur in our life-time.

Corporate leaders *always* seem to extol the virtues of their products and *always* seem to proclaim that the future growth of their companies depends upon improvements in the quality of the products that they offer and upon the characteristics of those products that give greatest satisfaction to present and future customers.

Some corporate leaders make this strategy of creating decisive consumer value explicit and explain the entire purpose of their enterprise in its terms. For example, John Smale, when CEO of P&G, was quoted by *Fortune* magazine:

> We first determine if we've got a technical right to succeed in a business. Then we look at the total size of the business and its profit margins.[1]

The idea that the only basis upon which a successful business may be built is one of technical superiority—of a better, more attractive product—is indigenous to the corporate culture of America. That it often comes a crop-per either because of the imperative of profit regularity or the bankruptcy of modern marketing, or both, has been demonstrated in Part I of this book.

What seems to happen sometimes is that corporate leaders lose sight of the importance of creating decisive value even as they publicly proclaim its importance. P&G apparently did not, after all, possess a viable "technical right" to succeed in their forays into the orange juice, non-cola soft drink, and packaged cookie businesses that were undertaken on Mr. Smale's watch. This does not mean that such technical rights had not been rationalized by P&G, for they undoubtedly had. What it does mean, however, is that for whatever reason, these ventures were greater or lesser failures simply be-cause the "technical right to succeed" did not, in the reality of the consumer marketplace, actually prevail.

Sometimes the idea of creating decisive consumer value seems to get lost in the perfection of technology for its own sake. Consumer-electronics products—VCRs; compact disc players; fax machines; telephone answering machines—have accumulated a dazzling array of technical features as each manufacturer seems to define competitive excellence in the refinement of technical performance as an end in itself. Whether this deluge of technical refinement—developed to provide obscure function—has any relevance to the mass of consumers never seems to enter into the product-development strategies of these companies. Technical refinement and proliferation of function justify themselves in the manufacturer's mind. Exhibit 12–1 shows 160 models of CD players as presented in a "necessarily very selective" listing that appeared in the *Stereo Review Equipment Buying Guide* for 1992.

ACCOUSTIC RESEARCH
CD–07 CD Player

ADCOM
GCD–575 CD Player

ARISTON
Ariston CD Player

AUDIO BY VAN ALSTINE
Omega CD Player

BANG & OLUFSEN
Continuous Music Module CD Changer
Beogram 4500 CD Player

CALIFORNIA AUDIO LABS
Aria mk III Hybrid CD Player
Icon mk II CD Player

CAMBRIDGE AUDIO
CD4 CD Player

CARRERA
CD–3400 6-Disc CD Changer
CD–3300R CD Player

CARVER
MD/V–500 Combi–Player
SD/A–490t Tube CD Player
SD/A–350 5-Disc CD Changer

CREEK AUDIO
CD 60 CD Player

DENON
DCD–3500RG CD Player
DCD–3560 CD Player
LA–3000 Combi-Player
DCD–2560 CD Player
LA–2000 Combi-Player
DCM–520 5-Disc CD Changer
DCM–420 5-Disc CD Changer
DCM–320

DUAL
CD–5150RC CD Player
CD–1070RC CD Player

FISHER
DAC–145 5-Disc CD Changer/Turntable
DAC–143 No turntable
AD–743 CD Player
DAC–7000 5-Disc CD Changer

HARMAN KARDON
HD 7600II CD Player
TL8500 5-Disc Changer
HD7450 CD Player
HD7400 CD Player

HITACHI
VIP RX6EX Combi-Player
DAC–70SW 12-Disc CD Changer
DAC501 5-Disc CD Changer
DA8200SW CD Player

JVC
XL–Z1050TN CD Player
XL–G512NBK CD+G Player
XL–M705TN 7-Disc CD Changer
XL–R304TN 5-Disc Changer
XL–R204TN No remote
XL–V241TN CD Player
XL–V141TN No remote

KENWOOD
LVD–300 Combi-Player
DP–M7730 7-Disc CD Changer
DP–R4430 5-Disc CD Changer
DP–5030 CD Player

LUXMAN
D–105U Tube CD Player
DC–114 7-Disc CD Changer
DZ–111 CD Player

EXHIBIT 12–1   "Necessarily very selective" listing of 160 models of CD players—1992

(Continued)

(Continued)

MAGNAVOX
CDV–305 CD Combi-Player
CDC552 5-Disc CD Changer
CDB502 CD Player

MARANTZ
CD–11 Mk II CD Player
CD–72 CD Player

McINTOSH
MCD 7007 CD Player

MELOS
CD–T Bitstream CD Player

MERIDIAN
Model 208 CD Player/Preamplifier
Model 206 CD Player

MITSUBISHI
M–V6021 Combi-Player
M–C4030 5-Disc CD Changer
M–C2050 CD Player

MOD SQUAD
Prism II CD Player

MUSEATEX
Melior CD Deck CD Player

NAD
Model 5000 CD Player
Model 5060 6-Disc CD Changer
Model 5425 CD Player

NAKAMICHI
CD Player 4 CD Player
CD Player 1 7-Disc CD Changer
CD Player 2 7-Disc CD Changer
CD Player 3 7-Disc CD Changer

NIKKO
NCD 2500R 5-Disc CD Changer
NCD 910R CD Player

NSM
CD 3101–AC 100-Disc CD Changer
CD 3101–H CD Player

ONKYO
Integra DX–708 CD Player
DX–C510 6-Disc CD Changer
DX–704 CD Player
DX–201 5-Disc CD Changer
DX–702 CD Player

OPTIMUS, BY RADIO SHACK
SCT–50 CD/Cassette Player
CD–6200 5-Disc CD Changer
CD–1760 CD Player

PANASONIC
LX–101 Combi-Player
SL–PC364 5-Disc CD Changer
SL–PG354 CD Player

PARASOUND
C/DX–98 5-Disc Changer
C/DX–88 CD Player

PHILIPS
CDV–600 CD Combi-Player
CDV–400 Combi-Player
Model 875 7-Disc CD Changer
CD–40 CD Player

PIONEER
CLD–3090 Combi-Player
CLD–M90 Combi-Changer
PD–TM1 18-Disc CD Changer
PD–7700 CD Player
PD–M650 6-Disc CD Changer
PD–M640
CLD–95 Combi-Player
PD–75 CD Player
PD–41
PD–M95 6-Disc CD Changer
CLD–731 Combi-Player

PROTON
AC–425 5-Disc CD Changer
AC–422 CD Player

QUAD
Quad 66 CD Player

QUASAR
LD500 Combi-Player
CD891 5-Disc CD Changer
CD831 CD Player

REVOX
H2 CD Player

ROTEL
RCD965BX CD Player
RCD955AX CD Player

SAMSUNG
CD–44R CD Player

SANSUI
CD–X711 CD Player
CD–X617 CD Player
CD–X211 CD Player
CD–3100M 5-Disc CD Changer
CD–2700 CD Player

SANYO
CPM510 5-Disc CD Changer
CP791 CD Player

SHARP
MVD–2000 Combi-Player
DX–C1800 6-Disc CD Changer
DX–200 CD Player
DX-R250

SHERWOOD
CDC-3010R 5-Disc CD Changer
CD–3010R CD Player

SONOGRAPHE, BY
CONRAD–JOHNSON
SD22 CD Player

SONY
MDP–333 Combi-Player
CDP–C910 10-Disc CD Changer
CDP–C715 5-Disc Changer
CDP–C615

CDP–C515
CDP–991 CD Player
CDP–491 CD Player
CDP–X777ES CD Player
CDP–X555ES CD Player
CDP–X222ES
CDP–C87ES 5-Disc CD Changer
CDP–C90ES 10-Disc CD Changer
CDP–C67ES 5-Disc CD Changer

SOTA
Vanguard CD Player

SYLVANIA
CD1552 5-Disc CD Changer
CD1502 CD Player

TEAC
AD–3 CD/Cassette Player
CD–P3000 CD Player
PD–D700 5-Disc CD Changer

TECHNICS
SL–P1300 CD Player
SL–PS900 CD Player
SL–PS700 CD Player
SL–PD807 5-Disc CD Changer
SL–PC505 5-Disc CD Changer
SL–PG300 CD Player

VECTOR RESEARCH
VCD–410R CD Player

YAMAHA
CDX–1050 CD Player
CDC–815 5-Disc CD Changer
CDC–715
CDX–750 CD Player
CDC–615 5-Disc CD Changer
CDX–550 CD Player
CDX–450 CD Player

ZENITH
LDP510 Combi-Player

Source: "1992 Equipment Buying Guide," *Stereo Review*, February 1992, pp. 72, 81–87.

In other instances the fault may lie in the way the purpose and character of the business has been defined by its executives. They seem to think of
the business in terms only of its physical reality and how that physical reality
has evolved, rather than in terms of the consumer satisfaction it creates.

Such narrow and inward-looking views of the ultimate meaning of the
business are well illustrated in the way that Alfred P. Sloan characterized the
business of General Motors during his stewardship:

> General Motors is an engineering organization. Our operation is to cut
> metal and in so doing to add value to it.[2]

The immediate reaction that one has to this statement of the General
Motors "purpose" is to raise the question: Add "value" for whom? Does
Sloan mean that the cutting of metal makes the metal more valuable to the
ultimate consumer, or does he mean that the cutting of metal itself increases
the price, including profit, that General Motors can ultimately sell the cut
metal for? If the first, then the company must be finally concerned with
what kind of cut metal its customers want. If the second, then it only need
be concerned with the most cost efficient and profitable way in which the
metal may be cut.

At the least, John Smale seemed to imply that the identification of the
"technical right to succeed" would not be solely made by P&G's engineers
and scientists. In fact, Smale's statement implies that the "technical right to
succeed" would only be granted in the competitive marketplace by the ultimate consumer.

Sometimes the importance of decisive consumer value seems to disappear in the roseate glow of corporate smugness and self-satisfaction. For
example, Alfred P. Sloan had this to say about the task of automobile product
engineering in 1964:

> In the course of time the product engineer raised the state of his art so
> high that he produced not only a superb creation but also a mature one,
> so far as the present type of gasoline-powered car is concerned. Now he
> devotes much of his skill to solving the problems created by the stylist.
> The consumer recognizes this today by taking for granted the varied en-
> gineering excellence of all competitive makes of cars, and so his shopping
> is strongly influenced by variations in style. Automobile design is not, of
> course, pure fashion, but it is not too much to say that the "laws" of the
> Paris dressmakers have come to be a factor in the automobile industry—
> and woe to the company that ignores them.[3]

By any standard this is a truly extraordinary statement. Set aside the fact that it is, as the last 35 years of automotive marketing have demonstrated, quite wrong. Anyone can be disproved by hindsight. Concentrate instead on the assumptions that Mr. Sloan has made about consumers.

The consumer "recognizes" that perfection has been achieved in the technical engineering of automobiles. The consumer "takes for granted" the "engineering excellence of all competitive makes of cars." The consumer "is strongly influenced" by the "laws" of fashion that have been developed by the Paris couturiers.

The plain and revealing truth of the matter is that Sloan, the accomplished engineer and organizer who had so much to do with the growth, accomplishment, and stunning success of General Motors as a business enterprise, simply did not know anything about the people who bought General Motors and competitive automobiles. But even such a lack of knowledge need not be fatal. There was no necessity for Sloan to know how the consumers of his time perceived value in automobiles, as long as someone with the overall responsibility for product-design decisions at General Motors *did know* on what basis those consumers perceived value in automobiles. The real problem with Mr. Sloan's statement is that he assumed that he knew what consumers were thinking when, in reality, he did not have a clue.

What we have is a wonderful example of a man secure in his knowledge of manufacturing processes, who is ignorant of the reality of marketing and of the necessary subservience of manufacturing process to what consumers believe or can be made to believe is good for them.

The point of all this is not to snipe at Mr. Sloan who, on the basis of his superb memoir, seems to have been quite beyond category in most of his interests and opinions. The point is to underscore the nature of marketing itself and to suggest, again, that the dilemma of marketing is caused by executives and, especially, by marketing executives who presume to speak for the consumer when, in fact, they do not know what they are talking about.

Acknowledging corporate rhetoric about how corporate growth in sales and profits must always depend upon product excellence and consumer satisfaction, we must recognize that there is a lot more to the strategy of providing decisive consumer value than mere protestations and promises. For the strategy to work there must be a real, informed, and continuing commitment to the creation of decisive consumer value, not mere guesswork and lip service.

Let us now turn to a classic example of American corporate dedication to the creation of consumer value—the development of Ford Taurus/Sable

automobiles that culminated in their introduction to the public in December
of 1985.

TAURUS/SABLE: HOW TO DEFINE DECISIVE CONSUMER VALUE

Around 1979, the Ford Motor Company decided to develop a new midsized
automobile that it intended to be decisively different and better than anything that its competitors could be expected to offer. Before such an automobile could be contemplated, Ford senior management realized that it was
necessary to understand explicitly the ways in which it thought about itself,
the ways in which it thought about automobile consumers, and the ways in
which it thought about building cars.

The problem for Ford, for General Motors, and for the rest of the
American automobile industry in the late 1970s was that it had misper-
ceived, for whatever reasons, the kinds of automobiles that Americans were
prepared and willing to buy. It was not only necessary for these companies
to reach a new understanding of American consumers and their perceptions
of automobile value, it was also necessary to revolutionize the entire process
of designing and producing automobiles so that new American automobiles
would, in fact, have characteristics that consumers themselves would
recognize as valuable. Ford was the only American manufacturer of
automobiles that was willing in 1979 to make this commitment and to accept
the considerable risk that it implied.

This commitment required no less than the development of a new set
of operational principles for the design and manufacture of American
automobiles. Ford, to its considerable credit and subsequent profit, consciously developed these new principles before actually beginning the development of what became, in 1986, the new Taurus/Sable automobiles.

What were these new principles of operation? There were at least five
of them:

1. Ford culture and Ford traditions were not relevant to the Taurus/Sable
   program.

   Ford could not develop Taurus/Sable as it had historically developed new automobiles. The traditions and culture that had evolved
   into the Ford way of designing and making automobiles were not attentive to consumer satisfaction, except in the most general sense of
   the term. Instead, these processes and practices were focused intern-
   ally on the craft of profitable automobile-making itself, instead of upon
   what consumers might come to recognize as valuable. This meant that

the Ford people listened too much to Ford people when they developed new cars and paid too little attention to the ultimate consumer.

2. It was possible to define what consumers would come to perceive as valuable in objective terms.

    Instead of paying lip service to excellence or thinking about it in general or global terms, Ford identified those characteristics that might serve as a basis of differentiation among automobiles. There were literally 400 specific characteristics so identified. Taken together, they could be used to define automotive value for American auto purchasers. Once identified, Ford then defined superior performance or function for each of these 400 characteristics.

3. A superior automobile is an integrated whole.

    The finished automobile, Ford reasoned, must rationalize all of these elements of potential excellence into an integrated whole. Thus, the whole automobile must represent, from an engineering standpoint, the most positive possible compromise among all of these individual characteristics of value. The more proactive this compromising process and the more integrated the whole, the more likely that consumers would view the car favorably.

4. There must be a new definition of the relation between consumer satisfaction and engineering competence.

    Ford recognized that the consumer could, at best, only verbalize likes and dislikes about individual design components in specific terms, but was incapable of synthesizing them into any final conception of a finished automobile product. It was the responsibility of the engineer to build a finished automobile that consumers would come to perceive as valuable. The engineer had to do this by finding engineering means to provide an integrated and final *automobile* entity that consumers would recognize as different and better than competitive automobile entities. This is vastly different from finding engineering means to create an integrated and final *engineering* entity. It is also different from blindly following what consumers say they want, regardless of the engineering consequences.

5. The development of a totally new car must command and subordinate all the resources of the corporation.

    Ford realized that the development of Taurus/Sable, if it were ultimately to be successful, must be perceived within Ford as an enterprise of the *total* corporation. This meant not only that the project must receive the necessary financial support, but also that it had to be given license to utilize all of the capital, physical, and personnel resources of the corporation to whatever extent and in whatever combination was necessary to guarantee success.

These principles implied an immense risk for Ford. The company intended to design and develop a new automobile in an entirely new way. This meant, to the extent the new principles were actually followed, that all the old ways of thinking and proceeding must be consciously perceived throughout the Ford organization as outmoded. This also meant that Ford had to come to the realization, as an organization, that it *could* and *must* consciously *will* the creation not of a totally new car but rather of a totally new *marketing entity* that happened to take the form of an automobile. It would be an automobile totally different from any automobile previously made by Ford.

No one at Ford could guarantee its success.

THE ORGANIZATION OF THE TAURUS/SABLE WORK

One of the most important characteristics of the Taurus/Sable project was that the work of various Ford departments that specialized in different aspects of the development of new automobiles was to be integrated and amalgamated.

The traditional means of creating a new automobile has always been a step-by-step process. Thus, the product planners developed a rather broad conceptual idea of the new car—its price class; the kinds of cars it would be developed to compete against; its general styling and performance characteristics; and so forth. Then the design engineers developed more formal, general specifications for the new auto as well as an idea of what it would look like in clay model form. Next the specifications engineers produced very detailed engineering descriptions of the new car that rationalized the conceptual automobile with the realities of actual manufacture. Then the clay prototype and detailed specifications were turned over to the manufacturing specialists who designed the actual processes through which the final components of the car would be manufactured and assembled. The finished cars were then turned over to the marketing department to be persuasively presented to the public.

These various functions as well as other peripheral functions had, traditionally, been carried out independently by each of the departments as they worked on their assigned task. That is, the work proceeded linearly from function to function with relatively little interaction between departments. Historically, the process had been rather loosely controlled as each step along the way proceeded within the standards and imperatives of individual departments and their employees.

The Taurus/Sable approach was to make the development process into a single, integrated whole with representatives of each of the individual developmental and marketing functions working together from the beginning of the process as an integrated and interactive group.

As *Business Week* reported:

> Team Taurus, however, took a "program management" approach. Representatives from all the various units—planning, design, engineering, and manufacturing—worked together as a group. The team took final responsibility for the vehicle. Because all of the usually disjointed groups were intimately involved from the start, problems were resolved early on before they caused a crisis.[4]

Not only did this integrative group approach resolve problems as they arose, it eliminated situations in which one functional group incorporated design or engineering elements into specifications or prototypes that had to be modified or eliminated, either unilaterally or confrontationally, by another group working at a later stage in the design/ development process.

TAURUS/SABLE: BEST IN CLASS

In order to make sure that the developed Taurus/Sable automobile was a recognizably superior product, Team Taurus identified, as previously noted, 400 features and characteristics of contemporary automobiles upon which consumer satisfaction might ultimately be based. After analyzing the performance of automobiles at, above, and below the anticipated Taurus/Sable price points on each of these characteristics, Team Taurus identified that feature or characteristic on a particular competitive automobile that exceeded the performance of all the other automobiles that had been analyzed. This automobile was rated "best in class" on this characteristic or feature.

The features or characteristics analyzed included individual attributes within such general categories as power train smoothness and performance; performance feel; driveability; ride; steering; handling; brakes; climate control; seat performance; operational comfort; and others.

The goal was to attempt to design for Taurus/Sable a version of each feature or characteristic that would equal or exceed the "best in class" standard. Ford believes that the first production Taurus/Sables met or exceeded these "best in class" standards in 80 percent of the 400 cases.

But it was not merely a matter of meeting or exceeding 400 individual performance or feature standards. In addition, the individual elements and indeed the cars as a whole had to be designed so that every feature and characteristic was compatible and synergistic with all the others. The interdisciplinary team that managed the development of Taurus/Sable was indispensable in making this interactive compatibility of all the features of the new automobiles a reality.

TAURUS/SABLE: THE INTEGRATION OF THE CONSUMER VIEW AND DESIGN REALITIES

Even with a streamlined and goal-directed organization and with an objective identification of the automobile characteristics that might seem decisively valuable to consumers, it was obviously necessary for Team Taurus to bring the ultimate consumer into the loop. Developing a working dialogue with consumers was considerably more complicated than simply going through the familiar motions of traditional marketing research. There were several reasons for this:

- In the first place, in a departure from traditional Ford custom, market research was not remote from the actual development of Taurus/Sable. Market researchers participated directly in the development of Taurus/Sable as *members of Team Taurus*.

    As Alton Doody and Ron Bingaman summarize, in their comprehensive study of the development of Taurus/Sable:

    > [Market researchers] ... were no longer oracles who passed along sacred edicts from the dizzying heights of World Headquarters. Working side by side with designers, engineers, manufacturing specialists, finance people, marketers, and other key operating personnel, they could become more sensitive to the complexities of putting an automobile together .... They were *team* members.[5]

- The focus of what the market researchers did in their work was also changed. The normal research process involves the extraction of information from consumers that is presumed to be both valid and relevant. As we have suggested in Chapter 10, such run-of-the-mill and traditional research focuses on consumer answers to questions as such. The market researchers dutifully report the answers they are given but have no further intellectual or career involvement with the information that they have supplied.

When market researchers personally participate in a product-design project, as in the case of Taurus/Sable, discrete answers to discrete and presumably relevant questions are considerably less important than the development of a visceral, instinctive, comprehensive understanding of how consumers perceive product features and the product as a whole. The researcher now must achieve enough understanding of the consumer so that consumer response to product innovations and elements can be anticipated and predicted at both the specific feature level and at the level of the car as a whole.

■ Finally, in the Taurus/Sable development process the market researcher was required to understand the engineering and financial constraints in the design process well enough to modify and interpret anticipated consumer reactions, prejudices, and desires in terms of what would ultimately be possible in the design process rather than merely desirable.

The ultimate success of marketing research in the Team Taurus project required that the researchers combine a penetrating understanding of the consumer with a complete understanding of what was practical and doable. This required an intensity and breadth of participation by the market researchers that has only rarely been achieved in American business. It gave the market researchers a bottom-line responsibility for the final effect of their work as a participant in the total Taurus/Sable development process.

The Taurus/Sable automobile that emerged from this process was, inevitably, a compromise between what the consumer wanted and what the producer could produce, as all new products are or should be. The difference in the Team Taurus approach was that these compromises were informed by a great deal of knowledge about the consumer as well as an intensive interaction of that knowledge and what was possible from the engineering standpoint in the perfection of the ultimate end product.

As Doody and Bingaman conclude:

It isn't enough, then, merely to listen to what customers are saying and to go with the flow. The Team Taurus approach is what might be called "creative listening."... The team knew that in order to put a world-class car on the American market it was impossible to satisfy every conceivable consumer preference.[6]

Neither would it be possible to ignore engineering innovations that consumers were unaware of or unable to fully comprehend. A case in point is the dramatically different styling that characterized Taurus/Sable. The physical contours of the cars were unlike any then available in the American market. There was considerable concern among Team Taurus members that the consumer would simply reject the styling configuration. Yet the appearance of the cars had much less to do with styling, as such, than with the wind resistance of the auto when driven. The Taurus/Sable configuration was designed to minimize wind resistance and thus to improve not only the driving characteristics of the car but also its fuel economy. The resulting body shape was adopted because it would result in an automobile of superior performance characteristics, in spite of how consumers might react to it.

At the same time, the innovation was not arbitrarily imposed upon consumers because it would be "good" for them or because "Father Ford in Detroit knows best," as had other design innovations been imposed in the past. Rather, Team Taurus went out of its way in marketing the finished auto to explain to potential consumers exactly why the cars looked as they did and the performance implications of that external design. In the end, the potentially controversial appearance of Taurus/Sable became one of the cars' most important attributes with consumers. What Taurus/Sable looked like turned out to be the look of the future for automobiles, both domestic and foreign. Exhibit 12–2 shows the original, 1986 Ford Taurus 4–door sedan and its intended competitor, the 1986 Chevrolet Celebrity.

This intense attention to the details of the automobiles produced from the joint standpoint of consumer and producer generated a marketing entity, in the full sense of that phrase, that was more calculated to cause consumer satisfaction than any automobile that had ever been designed by an American automobile manufacturer.

But this happy result was far from foregone. The entire Taurus/Sable program was, as mentioned above, one of inordinate risk for the Ford Motor Company. No matter how well-meaning or inspired a revolutionary product-development program like Taurus/Sable is intended to be, the ultimate performance of the product that it produces cannot be either foreordained or guaranteed. As Richard S. Tedlow has remarked, summarizing the ultimate challenge of marketing:

The customer disposes. But the company proposes.[7]

In the end, the Taurus/Sable program was an immense success for Ford: the cars sold very well, and the profits flowed as well. Ford was, in the

EXHIBIT 12–2   Ford Taurus Sedan—1986; Chevrolet Celebrity Sedan—1986

late 1980s, the most successful and profitable of all U.S. automobile makers. As the *New York Times* commented in 1991:

> Ford was sometimes portrayed as America's answer to Japanese auto makers, largely on the popularity of its midsized Ford Taurus and Mercury Sable cars, its growing market share, and its record profit.[8]

If the prospects for Taurus/Sable cars are, in 1993, somewhat less rosy than in the late 1980s, it is not because of any weakness in the original Taurus/Sable program. Ford's current problems appear to be based on its inability or unwillingness to make a timely update of the Taurus/Sable automobile—to repeat the original Team Taurus approach as promptly as the competitive environment in the American automobile market has seemed to require. Taurus/Sable received a face-lift in 1992, but no major redesign, apparently, will be accomplished until 1994, eight years after the original introduction of the cars.

If Ford has a problem today, it has perhaps been because of its inability to maintain and broaden the Team Taurus concept of automobile development beyond its initial success. Could Team Taurus really have been only a relatively isolated incident? Or does it represent a basic redefinition of the purpose of the company's activities? Is Ford still committed to the creation of decisive consumer value in automobiles, or was the Team Taurus concept a flash in the pan?

THE GENERAL MOTORS RESPONSE TO TAURUS/SABLE

If a revolution had indeed occurred at Ford, it was pretty much business as usual back at General Motors.

After the Taurus/Sable introduction early in 1986, the Ford share of the American automobile market moved from below 12 percent to about 15 percent by 1988. Meanwhile, as reported by the *New York Times*,[9] the market share of Chevrolet, the automobile brand most affected by the introduction of Taurus/Sable, dropped from 15 percent in 1986 to 11 percent in 1988. Ford had passed Chevrolet in market share.

In mid-1989, about three and one-half years after the introduction of Taurus/Sable, Chevrolet introduced the Lumina midsized sedan. As reported in the *New York Times*:

> For the General Motors Corporation and its Chevrolet division, the Lumina is more than just another family of vehicles. It is G.M.'s most

ambitious and far-reaching effort to regain prestige and a portion of the United States' market share it has lost since the early 1980s.

General Motors is not counting on technological wizardry or styling breakthroughs to win over customers from Ford. Rather, it is putting its hopes on an innovative marketing campaign that calls on Mickey Mouse and the rest of the Disney stable to sell the car.[10]

The new Lumina was, according to the *New York Times*, an amalgam of features drawn from other General Motors automobiles that were already on the road. In outward appearance, it was reminiscent of the Chevrolet Beretta and Corsica. Inside, the car was based on the GM–10 chassis and drive train that had previously been used in two–door coupes in the Pontiac, Buick, and Oldsmobile product lines.

The *New York Times* story continued:

... Chevy designers intentionally steered away from radically new styling because they did not want to risk alienating potential customers with untested designs that might be deemed ugly.[11]

All of this suggests there was little or no "creative listening" to consumers during the development of the new Lumina automobiles. General Motors clearly followed its traditional path in putting the Lumina together—gathering proven elements from existing automobiles and presuming that they would be good enough to satisfy the potential consumer.

Rather than pay much attention to the automobiles as such—no "Team Lumina," no "best-in-class" concept, no interactive marketing-research participation—Chevrolet depended instead upon the appeal of Walt Disney characters to pull customers to the Lumina. The reasoning was apparently that the Disney characters were so appealing to American consumers that they would attract the favorable attention of potential car buyers and validate the virtues of the Lumina as an automobile. Chevrolet also assumed some demographic identity between Lumina prospects and Disney enthusiasts:

But most of all, Chevy hopes to appeal to the type of families attracted to Disney Theme Parks, movies, and merchandise.[12]

What all this marketing hype had to do with Lumina automobiles remains obscure. What Chevrolet executives apparently conceived of as an "innovative" marketing program sounds more like a marketing pipe dream, replete with massive doses of contempt for the customer. It is our old friend, the myth that no matter what one does in marketing, advertising can always sell the product.

But even more indicative of the size and shape of the marketing funk into which Chevrolet's leaders had fallen was the revelation by Robert Burger, "recently retired General Motors vice president in charge of Chevrolet," that Chevrolet had committed the cardinal marketing sin of counting on sales to old customers to substitute for the creation of decisive, new consumer value. As the *Times* quoted Mr. Burger:

> Some people would say the Lumina doesn't excite them, and I know where you're coming from. The Lumina excites our dealers, it excites the leasing companies, it excites the segment of the market you need to sell 350,000 units annually.[13]

One is tempted to wonder whether Mr. Burger knew that consumers buy cars and drive them.

CREATING CONSUMER VALUE IN PROPRIETARY MEDICINES

Automobiles are large and complex pieces of machinery with, at any point in time, numerous opportunities for design changes and improvements. As the evolution of the automobile continues, it is evident that an automobile maker continues to have the opportunity to create new and tangible decisive consumer value just as Team Taurus did. But it may be argued that automobiles are a special case and that the opportunity to *will* decisive consumer value is much greater in this product category than, for instance, in consumer package goods.

There is certainly much merit in this argument. Common package goods have been proliferated, refined, and improved over many years. The proliferation of distinctionless brands and brand variants seems almost an admission of the inability of most manufacturers to create new and decisive consumer value in many package-goods product categories.

But the *will* to create decisive consumer value has less to do with the linear development of existing brands than it does with the attitude with which the corporation approaches the subject of its growth, and how this growth must come about. The distinction is clear when one compares the approach of Ford in the development of Taurus/Sable with the approach taken by General Motors in the development of Lumina. Not only did the

Lumina development program reflect a business-as-usual attitude at General Motors, it also reflected a studied indifference to the Taurus/Sable automobiles and their significance to ultimate consumers. And this studied indifference was not because General Motors lacked either the time or the resources for an aggressive response to Taurus/Sable. The Lumina introduction occurred three and one-half years after the first appearance of Taurus/Sable.

The essence of the creation of decisive, new consumer value is the existence of a *will* to do it. There is, for example, in the proprietary-medicine field a very broad opportunity to create decisive, new consumer value. This opportunity lies in the conversion of prescription drug products to over-the-counter medicines for unsupervised use in the home. Obviously, not all prescription drugs have the capacity for such conversion. But when a prescription product has been developed for the relief of common, easily identifiable symptoms of annoying but non-life-threatening physical conditions or disease, the Food and Drug Administration of the U.S. government provides an orderly process for use in considering the conversion of such prescription products to over-the-counter status. In recent years such conversions to over-the-counter status have occurred in several fields — in analgesics, decongestants, antihistamines, antifungals; and others.

For the proprietary-medicine manufacturer, the simple question is whether the business will grow as fast through the continued exploitation of existing over-the-counter products or whether it is likely to grow faster through the conscious process of finding prescription products that can be taken through the over-the-counter conversion process.

At one extreme, consider the case of the Glenbrook Laboratories division of Sterling Drug, Inc. It has not introduced one successful proprietary product that has been converted from prescription status in at least the last 40 years. It has, however, continuously managed and refined its Bayer aspirin brand. The trademark Bayer now appears on the following products: Genuine Bayer Aspirin; Bayer Plus Aspirin plus Stomach Guard; Extra-Strength Bayer Plus Aspirin plus Stomach Guard; Therapy Bayer Enteric Aspirin; Eight-Hour Bayer Timed-Release Aspirin; Genuine Bayer Aspirin Caplets; Maximum Bayer Aspirin; and Bayer Children's Aspirin. The current Bayer line is shown in Exhibit 12–3.

At the other extreme, consider the case of Schering–Plough and its Schering–Plough HealthCare Products division. Schering–Plough has a long history of converting prescription drugs to over-the-counter status, starting with Coricidin in 1951 and continuing with Tinactin in 1971, Afrin in 1976, Chlor–Trimeton in 1976, and Drixoral in 1982. In 1990, the HealthCare Products division was established to market the Schering–Plough proprietary-

EXHIBIT 12–3   Bayer aspirin brand variants—1992

medicine products including the prescription to over-the-counter brands that had already been established by Schering–Plough and to serve as a launching platform for the prescription to over-the-counter switches that were anticipated in the years ahead. Since the formation of this subsidiary, Gyne-Lotrimin (1990), Lotrimin AF (1990), and Duo–Film Products (1991) have been introduced. Presumably, other Schering–Plough prescription products are now in the Food and Drug Administration administrative process that will approve the conversion in status of some or all of these products in due course.

Exhibit 12–4 shows the eight products now marketed by Schering–Plough HealthCare Products that have been converted from prescription to over-the-counter status.

The driving force in this conversion process is the fact that successful prescription products have demonstrated, to the satisfaction of the medical community and the federal government regulators, a decisive value for unsupervised consumer use. Every prescription drug is judged by the regulators to be both safe (within the rules established for its use by the medical community) and effective for a particular human disease or condition. Subsequent acceptance of such governmentally-approved prescription products by the medical community indicates that they are more effective and/or more efficient and/or easier to take or use than other products that have historically been used to cure or relieve the indicated disease or condition. So in the case of such prescription products, decisive consumer value has already been demonstrated before conversion to over-the-counter status. The only question that remains for the Food and Drug Administration is whether these prescription products can be safely used by consumers without medical supervision.

It is interesting to note that in the conversion of prescription drugs to over-the-counter status, marketing research has little or no role to play in reconciling technology's capabilities and consumers' wants and desires. Drugs and medicines either cure or relieve diseases or conditions or they do not. If they do, decisive consumer value has been created. If they do not, no amount of creative compromising between technology and consumer wants and desires will change the situation.

IS THERE LIGHT AT THE END OF THE TUNNEL FOR OTHERS?

It is one thing to take a proven prescription-drug product and convert it to over-the-counter status by demonstrating to the Food and Drug

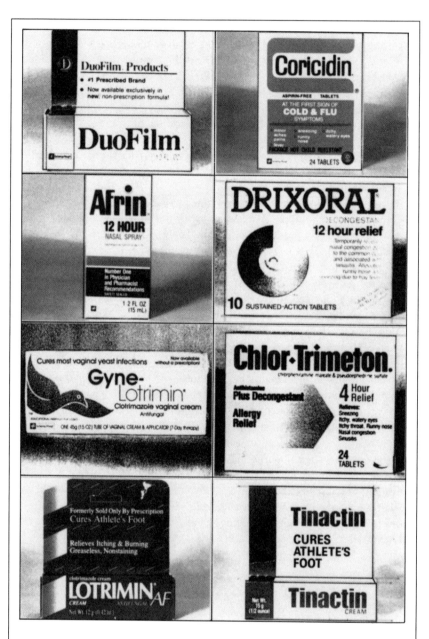

EXHIBIT 12–4   Schering–Plough HealthCare Products brands—1992

Administration that it is safe for unsupervised consumer use as an over-the-counter medicine. But does this mean that package goods are generally amenable to the value-creation strategy?

Certainly, leading package-goods manufacturers have not been conspicuously successful in creating decisive, new consumer value in recent years. The question is whether it is possible to do so. Are we really in the position where the only feasible "new" package-goods products are dis-tinctionless brand and brand-variant proliferations? There is no general answer to the question. It is, however, possible to describe at least one con-temporary new product that is characterized by decisive, new consumer value.

As we have seen, there is no shortage of brand proliferation in the bath bar-soap category. This category has been more or less stagnant for some years. Some brands contain moisturizing ingredients and may be said to be mild or gentle to the skin. Other brands have deodorizing properties. There are enough brands of both kinds to provide a kind of continuing com-petitive equilibrium in the category with generally stable market shares and an air of marketing torpor. Surely companies that market products in this category must have contemplated, at least in a relaxed way, the possibility of developing and marketing a bar soap that combines both moisturizing and deodorizing ingredients. To do so at a competitive price should create decisive, new consumer value for bath bar-soap consumers, or so it certainly seems.

Who knows what the obstacles to such a combination product may have been: Excessive cost? Technical difficulty? Internal, political bias against such a combination product? Marketing research that assures man-agement that such a product will fail? Smug satisfaction with existing prod-uct lines and their potential for growth? Preoccupation with existing market-ing thrust and parry among existing products? What else?

Whatever the obstacles to shattering the marketing equilibrium in the bath bar-soap category, and undoubtedly the obstacles must have at least *seemed* substantial, Lever Brothers has broken the impasse—and with con-siderable marketing success. Its new Lever 2000 (Exhibit 12–5) bar soap successfully combines both moisturizing and deodorant ingredients.

As *Business Week* reported,

> But just six months after its national rollout by Lever Brothers Co., ... Lever 2000 is the no. 2 deodorant soap in dollar volume, with an estimated 8.4 percent share of the $1.5 billion bar-soap market.[14]

Somehow or other, someone at Lever Brothers chose to will the cre-ation of a new product that would seem more valuable to consumers.

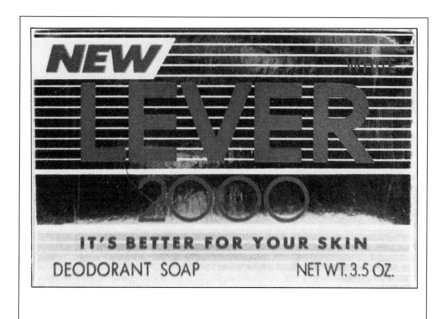

EXHIBIT 12–5   Lever 2000 bar soap

ONE OR MANY STRATEGIES FOR SALES AND PROFIT GROWTH?

It is important to note that the various marketing strategies for corporate growth in sales and profits that have been discussed are not mutually inconsistent. It is possible to accommodate the trade; increase marketing power through merger or acquisition; increase profits through the excision of brands or businesses; proliferate brands and brand variants; *and* attempt to create decisive consumer value, all at the same time. But, as already noted, not all of these strategies are likely to have the same impact on the long-term health of the corporation.

An interesting case in point is P&G, long regarded as one of the preeminent American marketing companies. The fundamental operating strategy of P&G has always been to find a distinguishing product characteristic— a "technical right to succeed" in a market—that will fetch a premium price because it offers the consumer decisive value. And there has been no apparent change in that fundamental strategy, even in recent years when

P&G has also adopted other, non-value marketing strategies for increasing sales and profits. The problem for P&G is that the "technical right" strategy has simply not been as dependably fruitful in recent years as in the past. As a former P&G executive vice president, Walter L. Lingle, has remarked:

... Product advantages are simply harder to come by today.[15]

It is presumably because of the difficulty of creating new bases of decisive consumer value that P&G has also embraced alternative strategies for achieving growth in sales and profits .

First of all, P&G has become an inveterate brand proliferator. We have already seen the proliferation of the Crest brand in Exhibit 3–5 and of heavy-duty detergent powders in Exhibit 11–1. There are many other examples. For instance, consider the proliferation of the Oil of Olay brand that is shown in Exhibit 12–6.

As *Fortune* magazine observed:

Since its lab couldn't bail it out the company has resorted to more plebian means to stanch the bleeding. It has introduced a series of unremarkable products that exploit existing brand names to capture shelf space and preserve market share. ... The company has also come out with "new" offerings that are nearly indistinguishable from existing products—for example, a powdered laundry detergent called unscented Tide (regular Tide with less perfume).[16]

P&G has also paid special attention to the accommodation of the trade as we have seen in Chapter 10. And it is not hesitant about getting out of unprofitable brands and businesses as its withdrawal from the Duncan Hines soft cookie and Orange Crush International soft-drink businesses suggests.

Nor has P&G been reluctant to acquire businesses in product categories in which the company senses an opportunity for growth. Sometimes such acquisitions have been particularly successful as in the case of paper products (Charmin Paper Company) and cold remedies (Richardson–Vick). In other instances the acquisitions have not fulfilled their apparent promise, as in the case of Orange Crush International.

Beyond all this, P&G has also attempted to extend its technological base by entering into partnership agreements with ethical drug companies such as Upjohn (for the development of baldness remedies); Syntex (for the development of anti-inflammatory analgesic substances); with the Dutch firm Gist–Brocades (for the development of ulcer treatments); and so forth.

EXHIBIT 12–6   Oil of Olay brand variants—1992

What P&G seems to be these days is a modern marketing company that will avoid no plausible strategy in its attempt to resolve the problems of contemporary marketing. The realization that a traditional consumer-value strategy may not provide all the growth in sales and profits that might be desired is certainly not unique to P&G. Many other consumer-product companies have found that it is not as easy to find new products of decisive consumer value as it was 20 or 30 years ago.

A major additional question is, of course, whether the consequent marketing thrashing-around is really as purposeful as it seems to be. Is the pursuit of decisive consumer value really proceeding with the same scope and intensity at a company like P&G today as it was say 30 years ago? Or do P&G and all of the other great marketing companies believe that all this marketing motion—and especially the motion of brand proliferation—is equivalent to or a substitute for the relentless pursuit of decisive consumer value?

At least some observers believe that companies like P&G and other great marketers have become complacent and have slackened off from the pursuit of decisive value because this pursuit is so expensive and increasingly difficult. Meanwhile the alternative strategies—brand proliferation, trade accommodation, business and brand trimming, accumulation of marketing power through merger and acquisition—are safer, easier, and less expensive.

That there may be a worm or two in the P&G apple is suggested by Danny Miller:

> P&G's parade of marketing victories—Crest, Tide, and Pampers to mention just a few—eventually left some of its managers with the distinct impression that they could sell the sizzle without the steak. To take advantage of its powerful marketing channels and reputation, P&G began to offer a proliferation of mediocre products.[17]

Have the major consumer package-goods producers in America confused marketing with marketing motion? It is no longer enough to pay lip service to the creation of decisive consumer value. What is required is a specific strategy for the creation of such value as a corporate activity. This corporate activity must be distinct from yet appurtenant to the ongoing marketing activities of the corporation. It is to this topic that we now turn.

[1] "Procter & Gamble's Comeback Plan," *Fortune*, February 4, 1985, p. 33.

[2] Sloan, Alfred P., *My Years With General Motors*, Doubleday & Company, Inc., New York, 1964, p. 248.

[3] Ibid., p. 265.

[4] "How Ford Hit the Bullseye with Taurus," *Business Week*, June 30, 1986, p. 86.

[5] Doody, Alton F., and Ron Bingaman, *Reinventing the Wheels*, Harper & Row, New York, 1988, p. 49.

[6] Ibid., p. 58.

[7] Tedlow, Richard S., *New and Improved*, Basic Books, New York, 1990, p. 375.

[8] "Ford's Pockets Are No Longer Full," *New York Times*, January 9, 1991, p. D-1.

[9] "Chevy's Answer to Ford's Taurus," *New York Times*, May 11, 1989 , p. D–1.

[10] Ibid., p. D–1.

[11] Ibid., p. D–1.

[12] Ibid., pp. D–l, D–8.

[13] Ibid., p. D–1.

[14] "Everyone Is Bellying Up to This Bar,"*Business Week*, January 27, 1992, p. 84.

[15] "P&G's Rusty Marketing Machine," *Business Week*, October 21, 1985, p. 112.

[16] "Procter & Gamble's Comeback Plan," *Fortune*, October 4, 1985, p. 32.

[17] The ICARUS PARADOX, copyright © 1990 by Danny Miller, p. 133. Reprinted by permission of HarperBusiness, a division of HarperCollins Publishers, Inc.

Chapter 13

Resolving the Dilemma of Marketing

The destiny of a corporation is determined by the marketing strategies that it adopts. All corporations become successful in the first place by offering some kind of unique and decisive value to the consumer. There are lots of ways that this initial success can be continued, but in the final analysis, mere perpetuation of past successes cannot guarantee continued profitable growth.

Continued prosperity depends upon the development of a succession of new marketing entities that offer the consumer decisive value. This value may be based on technology; access to scarce resources; innovative distribution; greater comparative quality; or illusions of value created by advertising. Whatever its basis, the corporation's long-term goal must be the continued creation of decisive consumer value.

This does not mean that the corporation should or can turn its back on its existing business or businesses, for of course it cannot. Rather, the issue is one of resource allocation. Some fraction of the corporation's resources must be set aside and dedicated to the creation of decisive consumer value. Presumably, the focus of this value creation will be on that business or those businesses in which the company is already actively engaged. But the idea of resource allocation to decisive value creation does not exclude ventures into new markets.

The key to success is a corporate understanding of what is ultimately involved in the creation of decisive consumer value. It does not mean a linear extension of existing businesses through dependence upon traditional research and development processes and arm's-length, disinterested market research. What it does mean is a conscious and calculated commitment to the creation of decisive consumer value as a distinct and separate corporate activity.

This commitment has organizational implications; strategic implications; and implications about the relevance of knowledge of the consumer.

THE NATURE OF MARKETING ORGANIZATIONS

One symptom of a continuing or expanded commitment to the creation of decisive consumer value is the creation of some sort of distinctive organization to facilitate the search for products and services that offer new or greater value to the consumer. This was certainly the case in the development of the Taurus/Sable; in the organization of Schering–Plough HealthCare Products; and it is true in other corporations that have become dedicated to continuous innovation in behalf of the consumer.

The major lesson that these corporations seem to have learned is that success with particular products or services tends to freeze organizations into the patterns of thought and operation that have caused this success in the first place. Such companies freeze in a lot of ways:

1. The basic organization chart does not change. More units may be added, but they are always organized in just the same way as other units within the company. Such organizations expand by adding new layers of authority—interspersing them among existing levels so that the organization can do what it has always done, only more so.

2. Organizations tend to freeze the kinds of information that are used to explore alternatives and reach decisions. The same kinds of statistics are generated by the sales and financial organizations year after year; the same kinds of tests are used to evaluate new products and new communication initiatives; the same kinds of financial tests and personnel evaluations are used to evaluate the progress of the corporation and its employees.

3. The strategic parameters and processes of the company are also frozen. Since the old strategies have served well in the past, there is no inclination to seek out or evaluate new or alternative strategies since on their face they will more often than not contradict or call into question strategies on which the success of the company has been built. As Danny Miller observes:

... The success of past strategies causes them to focus on just a few questions. Cost and design details, which had been the means to serve customers, become ends in themselves. This obsession creates resistance to change, an ignorance of markets, and a wayward marketing strategy.[1]

4. The same kinds of physical forms ranging from the design of buildings to the color of telephone message slips, are used in the organization for years on end. The physical environment thus perpetuates the idea that nothing can or should be changed because of the association that all of these physical forms have with the successes of the past.

5. Nor do the people in the organization change very much. The corporation draws its talent and labor pools from the same newspaper want ads, employment services, colleges, and graduate schools. Similar people continue to be recruited into the corporation. Meanwhile the rules of seniority are vigorously enforced so that the same kinds of personalities and work habits are promoted from within the corporation from year to year.

6. Finally, the American corporate zeal for cost cutting and periodic cost reviews tends to freeze the corporation into the ways of its past. Nothing is more threatening to the tender shoots of new corporate initiatives and corporate departures from the traditional than the program that squeezes out "waste" and cuts "fat" wherever it is sighted.

This continuing process of refinement and reinforcement of the existing ways guarantees that the corporation will continue, year after year, to perform and think more or less as it always has. The future is forever defined in terms of what has come before.

But the essence of successful marketing is the conscious creation of dissonance and disequilibrium. This means that successful marketing is based on a determination to introduce dissonance and disequilibrium into markets and a dedication to purposeful and meaningful change. Unless this dedication to flexibility, disequilibrium, and change can itself become institutionalized, the very processes and practices that first brought the corporation its success will tend to inhibit the corporation's ability to respond effortlessly to changing consumer values, changing markets, and marketing environments. One of the crucial causes of the problems of contemporary marketing is the inflexible corporate perpetuation of past practices and processes. The proliferation of brands and brand variants epitomizes such inflexibility and such infatuation with the past.

Thus, corporate responses to every situation or opportunity that presents itself become predictable. Marketing employees know exactly what to do because the accumulated wisdom of the corporate past tells them exactly what to do.

Past marketing success can become, therefore, the corporation's single most insidious marketing problem. As Danny Miller remarks:

> Success does two things. First, it reinforces and amplifies current strategic tendencies, often taking them to extremes. Second, it contributes to changes in leadership and culture in a way that supports and aggravates these excesses.[2]

The problem for many corporations is that success has not come about in a way that makes it self-regenerating. The success itself has been built on inflexible processes rather than upon processes that create their own opportunities for positive evolution.

One company that has institutionalized continuing innovation is 3M. For 3M the general strategy is, apparently, constantly to upset existing equilibrium in those markets where 3M can apply its expertise and impose its commitment to excel. The company encourages and rewards only innovation itself—a kind of non-strategic strategy. *Business Week* reports:

> ... 3M constantly finds itself playing host to companies trying to figure out how to be more creative ...

> While other companies may pick up ideas piecemeal from 3M, it would be impossible for any big corporation to swallow the concept whole. "We were fortunate enough to get the philosophy in there before we started to grow, rather than trying to create it after we got big," says Lester C. Krogh, who heads research and development.[3]

If the pursuit of decisive consumer value has not yet been made organizationally self-perpetuating, two things must be done:

- The company must recognize that as it is currently constituted it is not organized consistently to pursue decisive consumer value.

- The company must *will* organizational change that permits the consistent pursuit of decisive consumer value, while leaving the earning potential of the existing company intact, or reasonably so.

This is what Ford Motor Company did when it created Team Taurus. It is what Schering–Plough did when it created Schering-Plough HealthCare Products.

The point is *not* that the entire corporation must be reorganized. To the contrary, what must happen is that a fraction of a corporation's resources —personnel, financial, physical—must be set aside to deal with decisive, new consumer value. It is virtually impossible to create such dedication by asking members of the existing organization to deal with the creation of new value while they sweat and scamper to exploit existing businesses for increased sales and profits. What is not generally recognized in most corporations is that one marketing organization cannot be expected, realistically, to deal with both issues. Profit exploitation and the creation of new consumer value are different activities and they require radically different intellectual styles and strategic perspectives.

CREATING DISEQUILIBRIUM IN MARKETS

Once the corporation has committed itself as an organization to the pursuit of decisive consumer value, it must next focus on the processes that this new, stand-alone organization should develop to achieve this goal. There is little use in redefining the organizational structure unless there is also an inherent vision about what will be done with it.

First a decision must be made about where the new organization will focus its attention. The simplest way to say it is: *not on competition*. Competition provides the reference point for those in the corporation who seek ever-increasing sales and profits through the perpetuation of existing businesses. The focus of value creation should be, first and always, with the consumer and the consumer's satisfaction. It should be upon the means—technical, resource exploitation, distribution, quality, illusion, whatever—through which such consumer satisfaction can be created.

This is a point worth emphasizing. Too often, the creation of decisive consumer value is confused with the creation of decisive competitive advantage. This line of thought seems to run as follows: "If the guys who are beating us in the marketplace have a more modern plant, then we must modernize our plant facilities to make them the most modern in the industry." Or "if the guys who are beating us in the marketplace have the best technological development record in the industry, then we must spend whatever it takes to develop a superior technological capability for ourselves." And so on.

What this mental set leads to is the ultimate strategy of beating the competitor at the competitor's own game, whatever it may be. This is an attractive option because the competitors have shown that their successes are based upon their appeal to the consumer.

But this approach is flawed for two reasons:

- It does not necessarily lead to anything better than parity products. To mimic a competitor by doing what it does best does not automatically result in consumer perceptions that the resultant products or services have greater value than those of the pioneer.

- And there is no guarantee that the corporation can execute the competitive strategy with the same cost efficiencies and/or professional skill that the pioneer has achieved.

As Kenichi Ohmae observes:

Of course, winning the manufacturing or product development or logistics battle is no bad thing. But it is not what strategy is—or should be—about. Because when the focus of attention is on ways to beat the competition, it is inevitable that strategy gets defined primarily in terms of the competition.[4]

The alternative approach requires the corporation to adopt a strategy that develops products or services that are different from and better than those offered by the competition. It starts from the premise that the only effective way to compete in the long term is to explore purposefully those new, unusual, unanticipated approaches to product and/or service development that may be perceived by the consumer to offer greater value.

This is where the newly created organization comes into play. It is an organization that has been conceived to build new sales and profits by creating and exploiting dissonance in the markets that the corporation serves or wishes to serve. Such dissonance will drive the creation of decisive consumer value—that is, value that can be anticipated to be superior to the value that is offered by the competition rather than value that is merely at or below parity with the competitive goods and services.

The point is made by Richard S. Tedlow as he distinguishes the "beat the competition at their own game" option from what he calls the "strategic" option:

The strategic option ... is characterized by some new view of what the market wants or some new channel configuration to link manufacturer and consumer. When skillfully executed the strategic option can turn the incumbent's greatest strength against it.[5]

This determination to develop an alternative marketing entity that will provide decisive value to the consumer assumes both an organization that can make this determination come true and the will of the corporation to succeed in the venture. It also assumes a level of sophistication in the bed-rock marketing skills—product development, distribution, pricing, advertising, and promotion—to provide the process flexibility that the pursuit of decisive consumer value always requires.

As this alternative approach to corporate growth takes hold, it will inevitably call into question at least some of the contemporary marketing practices of the corporation. If, for example, the corporation's top management has embraced the concept of the creation of decisive consumer value and allocated corporate resources to implement it, is it not likely that this management will challenge the proliferation of distinctionless brands and brand variants? As the value-creation strategy permeates the thinking of the corporation, old non-value-based marketing strategies and initiatives must be called into question.

INVOLVING THE CONSUMER IN THE PROCESS

The value-creation strategy also assumes a determination to understand what the consumer *perceives* to be valuable. As we have emphasized before, this commitment to understand the consumer must be based on a willingness—one might say an obsession—to insure that the consumer can speak proactively. Thus, there must be an abolition of the "father knows best" kind of thinking—the endemic corporate hubris that insists that only the corporation itself knows what kinds of products or services will best serve the consumer.

And the determination to understand the consumer must be based on a willingness to ignore the apostles and intermediaries of conventional market research with their implicit presumptions about what the corporation *should* know about the consumer if decisive value is to be created.

Incidentally, just as it is crucial to isolate the marketing organization that will seek decisive consumer value from the marketing organization that will deal with competitive thrust and parry on a day-to-day basis, so it is crucial to isolate a marketing-research function within it. Marketing research that is concerned with the development of decisive consumer value and the valid prediction of what consumers are likely to perceive as valuable must abandon the processes and rituals of conventional market research practice. It was just such abandonment that made marketing research so important to Team Taurus and to the development of Taurus/Sable.

Until a way is found to create and train researchers to be true consumer surrogates in the creation of marketing and advertising entities the gap between what the corporation can provide and what the consumer really wants cannot be closed.

And it must be emphasized, there is plenty of risk in this process. If it is certain that conventional marketing research as it is organized and practiced has not been very good at anticipating positive consumer perceptions of value, all that can be said for an improved marketing-research process is that it *should* produce improved insights into what consumers will like. That improved process includes creative listening à la Team Taurus, and direct responsibility of the research for the validity and actionability of research findings. But the final value of the insights from this newly-conceived research process will still depend upon the ability of the individual researcher to become a true surrogate of the consumer.

So the value-creation strategy involves three distinct steps: the creation of an independent organization; the creation of a management point of view that is not obsessed with competitive gain as an end in itself; and a commitment to the development of valid market-research procedures that are placed in the hands of market researchers who have the innate skill to become true consumer surrogates and thus have the ability to predict how consumers will perceive positive value, no matter how difficult this may be.

In the end, it is the degree of validity of the corporate insight into the consumer that will define the exact corporate risk that is involved in attempting to please the consumer decisively. And this degree of validity can never be assumed as unequivocally certain.

THE ILLUSION OF DECISIVE CONSUMER VALUE

American marketers have long believed that advertising can, at its most inspired, create the marketing equivalent of a free lunch. That is, marketers have believed that it is possible to create the illusion of decisive consumer value even when the advertised product or service has little or no intrinsic difference from its competitors. But, as we have seen in Chapter 6, contemporary advertising is having the same problem in creating the *illusion* of decisive consumer value as marketers have had in creating the *reality* of decisive consumer value.

Advertising and other communication devices have increasingly been called upon to create the illusion of decisive consumer value as differences among products have declined and even disappeared. Advertising has a lot of problems at the moment, and perhaps some of them can never be solved.

But advertising should always have the capacity to make products seen different, if it is given half a chance.

We know that such subjective or psychological decisive consumer value can be created because it has been done in the past. The classic example is the psychological value that has been created, especially through advertising, for Marlboro cigarettes. Advertising and communication have been a powerful influence in creating the psychological value of the Kodak brand and its variants. Similarly, advertising has created enduring psychological value for BMW automobiles; Coca-Cola; United Airlines; Tide; Green Giant packaged vegetables; and other brands.

But as the Alka-Seltzer history in Chapter 6 suggests, opportunities for the creation of the illusion of consumer value through advertising may be transitory. There are indeed many brands and variants that have enjoyed only a short-lived illusion of decisive consumer value, profitable as such an illusion might have been in the short run. These brands and brand variants include, among many others, Smirnoff vodka; Dr Pepper; Aqua-fresh toothpaste; Chanel No. 5; Bisquick; the American Express Green Card; 7UP; Greyhound Bus Lines; Secret Deodorant; Avis Rent-A-Car; Federal Express; American Tourister Luggage; Lite beer; and so on.

What the past does demonstrate is that the illusion of decisive consumer value can be created by advertising, even if the illusion turns out to be relatively short-lived rather than enduring. It is, therefore, worth exploring the very real possibility that there are ways to improve the creation of the illusion of decisive consumer value.

THE ROLE OF THE ADVERTISING AGENCY

Creating the *illusion* of decisive value is even more difficult than creating the *reality* of decisive consumer value. Two organizations are involved rather than only one. Both the corporation and its advertising agency must participate in this process. But in advertiser–agency relationships the agency proposes and the advertiser disposes.

This suggests that unless the advertiser understands the importance and the nature of the value-creation process itself, it is unlikely that the advertiser and the agency will be able jointly to create enduring illusions of consumer value about the advertiser's products or services. This is so because advertising agencies can only sell those advertising ideas that their clients will buy. If clients do not understand the importance of the creation of decisive consumer value in their business, it is unlikely that they will understand or approve advertising that is created solely to project an enduring illusion of such value. But in addition, agencies will have little motivation to develop such campaigns—even if they are able—because they are unlikely to create advertising that they know their clients will not approve.

So it seems foregone that advertisers are unlikely to be exposed to, let alone approve, campaigns that have been explicitly developed to produce the enduring illusion of consumer value, *unless* the advertiser has already changed its own organization, strategies, and consumer orientations to ensure that it will create enduring consumer value.

Thus it seems obvious that the first requisite of creating the enduring illusion of consumer value is a client that buys the concept for its own business. Once this happens, it still remains for the agency to put its own house in order. Advertising agencies that are in the business of creating advertising their clients will buy are not necessarily in the business of creating advertising that will cause enduring illusions of decisive consumer value. The fundamental intellectual and strategic processes are simply different. Changes will have to be made within the agency. The changes that are required are, not surprisingly, the same kinds of changes that corporations themselves must make in the pursuit of decisive consumer value: changes in organization; changes in strategic perception; changes in the extraction of information from consumers.

ORGANIZING ADVERTISING AGENCIES TO CREATE THE ILLUSION OF VALUE

Advertising agencies are now organized to serve their clients through four basic departments: the contact department; the creative department; the media department; the research department. The contact team interfaces simultaneously with the client on the one hand and with the other agency departments on the other. The contact team is supposed to develop a deep knowledge and understanding of its client's business, ultimately becoming a full marketing "partner."

The contact team, informed by the marketing actualities and complexities of the client's business, is then responsible for directing the work of the other agency departments to assure that the advertising they create and the media in which it appears generate full advertising end-value. This organizational structure nurtures an ongoing process of advertising development that is highly responsive to the day-to-day marketing activities and needs of the client. It is, therefore, both subordinate to and responsive to marketing practice as usual. The agency's objective is only to create advertising that the client will like and approve no matter what illusion, if any, it may create in the minds of the consumers who are exposed to it.

If advertising agencies are consistently to create illusions of decisive consumer value in behalf of the clients for which they advertise, they must organize themselves to do so. And this means the creation of a separate organization that does not concern itself with the hurly-burly of day-to-day marketing and the advertising decisions that it generates. In other words, the *agency* must organize itself to create consumer value in much the same way that the *advertiser* organizes itself to create consumer value—by isolating value-creating activities from marketing activities that respond to day-to-day competitive thrust and parry. As emphasized above, agencies have little reason to create such organizations unless and until their clients have embraced a value-creation strategy in their own organizations.

But once this happens and the agency's consumer-illusion, value-creation organization is in place, it remains to define value creation in terms of the illusions that advertising can create for specific, individual products and services and to focus on the reform of the consumer-research processes that will inform the creation of such advertising. As agencies adapt themselves and their research processes to the value-creation strategy, they will do exactly the same things that their clients have done in developing value-creation organizations to produce products and services that will seem decisively valuable to consumers.

Leo Burnett, founder of the advertising agency that bears his name, created or supervised the creation of an unprecedented number of advertising campaigns that imparted an enduring illusion of decisive consumer value. Most of this extraordinary work was done in the 1950s and 1960s. The most outstanding example is the campaign in behalf of Marlboro cigarettes. But there are other enduring illusions of product value from the same period: the Jolly Green Giant campaign; the Friendly Skies of United Airlines campaign; the You're in Good Hands with Allstate campaign; the Tony Tiger Frosted Flakes campaign; the Charlie the Tuna Star–Kist campaign; and others.

In fact, Leo Burnett as copywriter and creative supervisor seems to have created or been associated with more enduring illusions of decisive consumer value than any other advertising practitioner before or since.

Perhaps we should simply say that Burnett was a genius, sigh deeply, and let it go at that. But as the quotation in Chapter 6 suggests, Burnett had clearly-articulated, creative methods. Perhaps the challenge to the creative practitioners of advertising is to study those methods—or the methods of anyone else who has created enduring illusions of decisive consumer

value—with the objective of institutionalizing these methods and per-
petuating them.

Surely such a study of creative methods would not merely rediscover
the ways that advertising agencies now use to create campaigns that can be
sold to advertising clients and campaigns that can be kept sold. Likely these
methods of creating enduring illusions would be at once less complicated
and far more subtle than those currently in use. They would be much less
dependent upon the arcane methods of arm's-length and indifferent marketing research. They would be much more dependent upon a directed personal interaction between the creator of advertising, either directly with
consumers or with consumer-researcher surrogates of consumers.

Of course there is the risk of failure in the search for new methods of
creating enduring illusions of decisive consumer value, just as there are risks
in the institutionalization of methods for creating tangible, decisive consumer value. But the future of advertising, just as the future of marketing,
must rest with the creation of decisive consumer value and nothing less. The
marketing issues of our time are how to identify decisive consumer value,
how to create it or its illusions, and how to perpetuate it.

THE MARKETING CONCEPT, YET AGAIN

The marketing concept means that the objective of corporate activity is to
create satisfied customers.

In the first part of this book, we reviewed the recent history of marketing and the myths that have driven it to the strategy of brand and
brand-variant proliferation. Brand and brand-variant proliferation does not
take as its objective the creation of a satisfied customer. It takes as its objective the creation of incremental sales. Brand and brand-variant proliferation
as marketing strategy is neither based upon nor reflective of the marketing
concept.

Nor are other currently-popular marketing strategies either based
upon or reflective of the marketing concept. These are the strategies of trade
accommodation; building marketing power through mergers and
acquisitions; and the elimination of unprofitable brands or businesses. All of
these strategies may improve sales or profits, at least in the short term, but
they are not likely to create consumer satisfaction.

If it is true that branding is at the heart of the American market economy, and I believe that it is, it is necessary to have a clear view of what
brands have meant to marketers of the past.

Brands were first created as a simple warranty of consumer satisfaction. It is thus through brands that the marketing concept has historically been realized.

Present-day marketing falters because it is dedicated to the dilution of brand meaning. Brands no longer have the certain power to provide a warranty of consumer satisfaction. As brands are proliferated and manipulated, their ability to create consumer satisfaction is diminished. Meanwhile, alternative, outward-looking marketing strategies may create sales but do nothing to create consumer satisfaction.

As this evolution has taken place, the marketing concept has deteriorated into a sales obsession. The idea of consumer satisfaction, no matter how important it has been for marketing in the past, has too little meaning in the marketing practice of the present.

Coincidentally, American marketers have come to value survival above all else. So far, survival—especially short-term survival—has been relatively easy to achieve. But the only way to guarantee the future is to focus on the development of marketing entities that create new consumer satisfaction. The trick is to maintain competitive presence while simultaneously adopting a value-creation strategy. This is the only way that the corporation can be sure to survive in the short term and prosper in the long term.

To really "grow the business" and to create bounteous future profits, it is necessary to take the risks that are associated with change; with reorganization; with the pursuit of competitive advantage through new knowledge; and, in the end, with the creation of dissonance and disequilibrium in consumer markets. That is the way that valuable new things—concepts, products, services, whatever—come into being, including decisive consumer value, tangible or illusory.

As Peter Georgescu has observed:

In American business today, *added value* is the only viable road to continuing growth and prosperity.[6]

What remains is the need for corporate will to create decisive consumer value. More of the same old marketing tricks will not do the job. More of the same old organizational processes and attitudes will not do the job.

What is required is a hard-boiled determination to change the corporate way of doing things so that the customer *will* be better served, no matter how fraught with risk this road may be.

[1] The ICARUS PARADOX, copyright © 1990 by Danny Miller, p. 42. Reprinted by permission of HarperBusiness, a division of HarperCollins Publishers, Inc.

[2] Ibid., p. 32.

[3] "Masters of Innovation," *Business Week*, April 10, 1989, p. 63.

[4] Reprinted by permission of *Harvard Business Review*. "Getting Back to Strategy," by Kenichi Ohmae (November/December 1988), p. 149. Copyright © 1988 by the President and Fellows of Harvard College, all rights reserved.

[5] Tedlow, Richard S., *New and Improved*, Basic Books, New York, 1990, p. 368.

[6] Georgescu, Peter A., " 'Back to School'—Advertising as a Productivity Force," address to the Chicago Advertising Club, February 17, 1988, p. 23.

Afterword

As we have seen, many business realities have contributed to marketing's contemporary problems:

- The inability or unwillingness to create distinctive new products and services

- The long-term decline in the creativity of advertising

- The emergence of the retailer as a power in influencing consumer brand choice

- The failure of marketing to create genuine brand loyalty

- The misdirection of corporate progress that is inherent in the brand-management system

Each of these conditions is enough to cause and perpetuate the problems of contemporary marketing. Yet even more, these problems are caused by a business attitude that is both pervasive and insidious. The attitude is simply stated:

"If I make my numbers, I've done my job."

This attitude ensures that the present will be perpetuated at the expense of the future. In the end, it will destroy the creation of marketing entities that attract customers and make them come back.

In the end, it may destroy considerably more than that.

Index

TITLES OF INTEREST IN MARKETING, DIRECT MARKETING, AND SALES PROMOTION

For further information or a current catalog, write:
NTC Business Books
a division of *NTC Publishing Group*
4255 West Touhy Avenue
Lincolnwood, Illinois 60646-1975 U.S.A.